The Grand Strand

An Uncommon Guide to Myrtle Beach and Its Surroundings

Nancy Rhyne

The East Woods Press

Copyright 1981, 1985 by Fast & McMillan Publishers, Inc.

Second Printing, 1985

All rights reserved. No part of this book may be reproduced without permission from the publisher, except by a reviewer who may quote brief passages in a review; nor may any part of this book be reproduced, stored in a retrieval system or transmitted in any form or by any means, electronic, mechanical, photocopying, recording or other, without written permission from the publisher.

Library of Congress Cataloging in Publication Data

Rhyne, Nancy, 1926-
  The Grand Strand.

  Bibliography: p.
  Includes index.
  1. Myrtle Beach, S.C. — Description — Guide-books. 2. Myrtle Beach region, S.C. — Description and travel — Guide-books. I. Title.
F279.M93R49   917.57'87   84-72966
ISBN 0-88742-053-2

Cover design by
Typography by Raven Type.
Printed in the United States of America by Edwards Brothers, Inc.

An East Woods Press Book
Fast & McMillan Publishers, Inc.
429 East Boulevard
Charlotte, NC 28203

About the Author

Nancy Rhyne's residence is Myrtle Beach, South Carolina. She has researched and written articles for many publications, including *The New York Times, Town & Country, Sandlapper, The Charlotte Observer* and *The Charlotte News*. Her other published books are CAROLINA SEASHELLS, TALES OF THE SOUTH CAROLINA LOW COUNTRY, and MORE TALES OF THE CAROLINA LOW COUNTRY. She is working on a modern plantation novel and a guide to haunted places on the coast of the Carolinas and Georgia.

Nancy Rhyne

Photo by Penny Christensen, Courtesy *Pawleys Island Perspective*.

Foreword

There are several groups of readers who will find enjoyment in this book. The first group is perhaps the smallest. It consists of that handful of natives and long-time residents who will enjoy seeing on the printed page the stories their parents and grandparents have told them. They will be fascinated by the way in which Nancy Rhyne has captured the facts and the flavor of lowcountry life during the formative period of the Myrtle Beach area. Many of them will feel a close identity with the names and the legends that, heretofore, have existed only in the spoken word.

The second group of interested readers will be only slightly larger than the first. That group will be made up of about half of the area's permanent population of fewer than 50,000 people. These 25,000 residents have moved to the area in the last ten years in search of a better climate, a better life-style or employment opportunities. Finding these, they have begun to develop an intense interest in the history and geography of the area. This book will help them to establish their roots and to enjoy being a part of this special section of America.

The last group of readers is, by far, the largest. It consists of more than seven million annual visitors to South Carolina's Grand Strand. These visitors come to our community with a variety of interests, and many fall in love with the area. They search libraries and other sources for information about the area, but find only bits and pieces. Nancy Rhyne's efforts in writing this book will be appreciated by thousands who will use it both as a guidebook and as a history book. They will enjoy her writing style, and they will appreciate the fact that so much of the information they seek is contained within the covers of a single publication.

Our visiting public is diverse. Quite often, a first visit is the result of reading a magazine or newspaper advertisement extolling "fifty miles of unspoiled beach" or "more than three dozen golf courses." Visitors who come to our community in pursuit of a single recreational interest are surprised and pleased by the diversity of opportunity they find here. Perhaps this explains why more than 70 percent of all first-time visitors pay a second visit to the area during the following 12 months. Perhaps this is also why so many of them come into our Chamber of Commerce offices seeking answers to questions and directions to some little-known spot on our coast.

Myrtle Beach is a paradox. It is little known to much of the country, and yet it is one of the leading vacation destinations on the East Coast. The neon lights of the amusement areas are dreamed about by youngsters who are yet to learn about George Washington or the Lords Proprietors. Golfers who traverse the thousands of acres of lush fairways are unaware of the magic that the digging of the Intracoastal Waterway performed on what had been known as the "impassable swamp." Visitors browsing through the quaint shops of the area are oblivious to the drastic changes that have taken place here during the past 300 years.

This book will provide these diverse groups of readers with a better understanding of South Carolina's Grand Strand. It will provide answers sought by residents and visitors who are attempting to explore their new-found vacation paradise.

Many will be grateful to Nancy Rhyne for the countless hours she has spent searching archives for bits and pieces of information; for the effort she has expended in locating and identifying musty old pictures that survived the albums and attics of a humid climate; and for the perseverance she has exhibited in seeking out and questioning the few remaining residents who have first-hand knowledge of the area's transition from swampland to glittering resort.

This is an excellent guidebook to the history and landmarks of the area known as "Myrtle Beach and South Carolina's Grand Strand." You will enjoy the book . . . and the area.

Ashby Ward
Executive Vice-president,
Myrtle Beach Area Chamber of Commerce

Preface

While researching the history of Horry County for the University of South Carolina Press, I became intrigued with that development that lies spread before us from Little River to Georgetown—the Grand Strand. We had owned a house at North Myrtle Beach for 15 years and had vacationed here during each of the 12 months (we now live year-round in the Ocean Forest section of Myrtle Beach), but never before had I seen, as a stranger might, the beauty and quaintness of this coastal place.

As I traveled the roads of Horry and Georgetown counties looking up old-timers and descendants of people who lived at this place generations ago, I came upon many tourists who were searching for just such a book as this. There was a man at the counter in the office of the Myrtle Beach Area Chamber of Commerce one rainy day asking for directions to places of historical significance. And Tom and Rose Zito of Bayonne, New Jersey, asked at the Myrtle Beach Hilton for a book on the history of the Grand Strand as they golfed away a January week. Then there were the people who left their yacht at a marina on the Intracoastal Waterway and struck out seeking a guidebook on Myrtle Beach—and a laundromat.

In telling the Grand Strand story, it is my intention to describe in the manner of a guidebook villages, towns, museums and attractions, some of which have been little altered in 100 years and more. But restraint has been necessary in the telling because no coastal area in this nation has a greater mass of historical tradition and folklore. Much of the region's charm lies in its legends and romance, traditional beliefs and customs. I have endeavored to give you, the reader, a glimpse into that time when Old South moonlight and magnolias were more than a legend.

As manifestly impossible as it is for me to thank adequately some of the people who helped me obtain the history and stories that follow, I call attention to the use of facilities and services of the Archive of Folk Song, Library of Congress. I am especially grateful to Pat Markland and Gerry Parsons. Genevieve Willcox Chandler fired me with her enthusiasm for the people of the coast of South Carolina, and those of her stories not told to me at her home in Murrells Inlet were obtained from material she had recorded and sent to the Library of Congress.

I am especially grateful to Gurdon L. Tarbox, Jr., Director of Brookgreen Gardens, for the many ways in which he helped with facts and photos. He also put me in touch with others who spent hours talking into my recorder. Edwin O. Fulton of Wachesaw Plantation gave me the story of rice cultivation and much, much more.

Also, thanks are due to the following: Catherine H. Lewis, librarian, Horry County Memorial Library; C. B. Berry, surveyor, historian and writer, of Crescent Beach; Mark E. Abbott, TSgt. USAF, Myrtle Beach Air Force Base; Ella Severin, Sue Mushock and Rachel Thomas of Hobcaw Barony; Olive Mancill of Georgetown; John M. J. Holliday of Galivants Ferry; Edwin Craig Wall, Sr., of Conway; Marion Culp of South Carolina Department of Parks, Recreation and Tourism and Jean Meyers (D—Horry), member of South Carolina House of Representatives and South Carolina Coastal Council.

Much gratitude and appreciation is due Warren Johnston and the staff of the *Pawleys Island Perspective* for the beautiful photographs they provided.

Others who helped so abundantly include Dr. Charles Joyner of Coastal Carolina College; Tim Hewitt of Paperback Booksmith at Myrtle Square Mall; Nate Shulimson of the Book Shoppe at Village of the Barefoot Traders; A. H. "Doc" Lachicotte of The Hammock Shop; Dr. Chalmers G. Davidson, archivist, E. H. Little Library at Davidson College; Chris Beachley, owner of The Wax Museum, a Charlotte, North Carolina record shop, and publisher of *It Will Stand*, a magazine devoted to Beach Music; Charles A. Milstead of International Paper Company; H. H. Bailey, Jr., of Georgetown Steel Corporation; Robert L. Joyner, project leader and resident biologist of Tom Yawkey Wildlife Center; Ashby Ward, executive vice-president of Myrtle Beach Area Chamber of Commerce; Justin Plyler; Rosemary Lands; Debbie Miller; and a southern lady in the truest sense, Miss Florence Epps. A happy by-product of writing a book is the people one meets.

Now I come to those who helped guide me through the putting together of this book. No author could ask for more sage and sensitive counsel than was given by Sally Hill McMillan and Barbara Campbell of The East Woods Press.

But above all, I do want to say how lucky I feel to have had the support of my husband, Sid. He saw that there was always a tape in my recorder, drove the car on back roads as I searched and researched, made photocopies by the hundreds at the Library of Congress, and photographed many of the scenes in the pages ahead. Without his help, I might still be typing page one.

Photo by Penny Christensen. Courtesy of *Pawleys Island Perspective*.

For Sid

Know ye the land where the cypress and myrtle
Are emblems of deeds that are done in their clime?
Where the rage of the vulture, the love of the turtle,
Now melt into sorrow, now madden to crime!

Lord Byron

Contents

Introduction 13
Little River 17
Cherry Grove Beach 21
Ocean Drive Beach 23
Crescent Beach 25
Atlantic Beach 29
Windy Hill Beach 31
Meher Spiritual Center 33
Intracoastal Waterway 35
Singletons Swash 37
Myrtle Beach 39
Myrtle Beach State Park 51
Myrtle Beach Air Force Base 53
Surfside Beach 57
Garden City Beach 59
Murrells Inlet 61
Brookgreen Gardens 67
Huntington Beach State Park 77
Sandy Island 81
Litchfield Beach 83
Pawleys Island 85
Debordieu Colony 91
Hobcaw Barony 93
Georgetown 95
Tom Yawkey Wildlife Center 103
Socastee 105
Conway 107
Bucksport 111
Galivants Ferry 115
Bibliography 118
Index 119

Photo by Penny Christensen. Courtesy of *Pawleys Island Perspective*

Introduction

The South Carolina Grand Strand extends 60 miles from the North Carolina state line at Little River to Georgetown at Winyah Bay. The arc of shoreline is named Long Bay, and Horry (OH-ree) County covers the northern 35 miles. The southern length of 25 miles is in Georgetown County.

Horry and Georgetown Counties

Horry County is named for Peter Horry, who served as a colonel under Francis Marion in the Revolutionary War. It is the largest county in South Carolina, comprising one twenty-seventh of the state's total area. In this county a person can go to the best of New York theatre or listen to spirituals sung by descendants of the enslaved songwriters. In this county a granny woman can be hired to deliver a baby, or a patient can be treated by nuclear medicine. On maps of this county a name is shown for a place that has only a live oak tree to mark the spot. The county may have 350,000 visitors present at one time, reflecting expenditures of millions of dollars in a single day. Although it draws more visitors today than any other county in the state, Horry was one of the last areas in South Carolina to be opened to civilization. Surrounded by rivers, swamps and ocean, it was called "the independent republic of Horry."

Geologists say that aeons ago Horry County was under water. John M. J. Holliday of Galivants Ferry (approximately 32 miles west of the seashore) agrees: "There is no doubt in my mind that thousands of years ago this was the edge of the ocean because the land here goes down pretty quickly and it is quite easy to find sea shells in this area." Indians were the first to live here, then the Spanish came, and they were followed by the English.

About the middle of the 1800s, most of the people of Horry County worked in large tracts of pine woods. Horry County residents were described as being poor and primitive, while their neighbors in Georgetown County reached a peak of power, wealth and influence.

Georgetown County, named for King George II who granted

The Grand Strand

the land for settlement, used her lowlands during this period to produce almost one-fourth the amount of the national rice crop. The rivers that rose and fell with the tides were perfect for flooding the rice fields, as salt water did not invade the tidal water this far from the ocean. In addition, an ample labor force for rice production was at hand.

History has recorded a few wealthy Horryites with inventories of a large number of slaves, but for the most part the people were unaccustomed to plantations or large land holdings, unlike the planters in Georgetown County. Consequently, the people of Horry formed their own self-reliant standards and held onto their lowcountry trump card, which they would play 100 years later.

Tobacco and Lumber

The first tobacco warehouse in Horry County opened in 1899, and the industry thrives to this day. (Horry ranks first in tobacco production of counties in the state and ranks as sixth in the nation.) Testimony to the lumber industry that still flourishes are hundreds of trucks loaded with pines on the way to sawmills. Tar kilns found throughout the county are believed to have been built in the 1850s when forests emerged as centers in the timber industry. Although many of the pines were cut by Henry Buck in the 1800s when he operated three large sawmills on the Waccamaw, in the earlier part of this century one could hardly tell that the forests had been touched. Edwin Craig Wall, Sr., chairman of the board of Canal Industries, has said, "When I came to Horry County in 1935, it looked like heaven to me. I had never seen such beautiful timber in my life." Despite the success in the yield of tobacco and pine lumber, still beyond the horizon was what was to become the major industry of the county and state—tourism.

Tourism Comes to the Grand Strand

In 1900 a little train named Black Maria conveyed passengers from Conway to the coast, and interest in the strand was sparked. Horry County played her trump card after World War II when two major highways and two airports accommodated beach visitors. The Grand Strand experienced almost unequaled growth. Rivers, marshes and coastline, once accused of isolating the country, were suddenly considered to be her major natural assets. Total transient accommodations on the Grand Strand

Introduction

today are more than 200,000, and 36 million accommodations have been used in a single year. The 1980s began with a season that brought in over $700 million, a 9 percent increase in business over the previous year. The county whose people were once called poor and primitive today has the town with the highest per capita income of any city in South Carolina—Myrtle Beach.

The quiet elegance of the Georgetown County portion of the Grand Strand is evident almost at the county line beyond Garden City Beach. One hundred and thirty years after rice planters brought attention to the land of moss-drenched oaks and rivers with tides that rise twice every 24 hours, this part of the strand prospers on understatement. Some of the beaches are surprisingly uncrowded. True lowcountry natives still go to the Episcopal churches the planters attended. And they do not buy a plantation on the Waccamaw, Pee Dee, Black and Sampit rivers. They inherit one.

The days when most of the Grand Strand's more than 45,000 motel rooms and apartments are filled and when a camper is hooked up on each of the more than 10,000 campsites are from June 1 through Labor Day, but visitors come in record numbers during other times as well, and some of them come to stay.

It is a fact that large numbers of people who choose the Grand Strand as their retirement home find the very mild seasons more to their liking than the steady warmth of southern Florida. Also, housing and living costs are somewhat lower than in some other parts of the country, and there is no local sales tax. State tax is five percent. Not the least of the reasons why retirees are lured to the Grand Strand is the homestead exemption, which allows homeowners 65 or older to exempt the first $15,000 value of their home and land from county and special assessment taxes. The city of Myrtle Beach also allows an exemption of $15,000 on the value of their home. "We find increasing numbers of people who visit [the Grand Strand] set their sights on retiring here," Ashby Ward says. "As a matter of fact, 28 percent of the people who locate here are coming to retire." *Money* magazine has ranked South Carolina third among the best states for retirees, and more military retirees settle in this state than in most states.

Each March, traditionally during the time of a school break in Canada, Canadians come to the Grand Strand by the thousands. Late March is better known as Canadian-American Days or the Can-Am Festival, and the flag with a maple leaf flies beside the

The Grand Strand

Stars and Stripes over many motels and other businesses. Merchants give the Canadians special prices and attention.

Hundreds of Scandinavians visit the Grand Strand in the fall, and beach officials expect this migration to become as regular as the Can-Am Festival in spring.

The Sun Fun Festival, held each June, is the largest annual event of its kind in South Carolina. The festival features beauty pageants, arts and crafts shows, parades, tours of historic areas and industrial sites and vacationer competition in all kinds of contests.

The *Accommodations Guide,* a free, detailed listing of available rooms, apartments, villas, cottages and campsites, can be obtained by writing to: Myrtle Beach Area Chamber of Commerce, P.O. Box 2115, Myrtle Beach, South Carolina 29577.

COAST magazine is the motel/hotel magazine of Resort Publications and is available in all leading accommodations, restaurants and fine shops on the Grand Strand.

The Grand Strand is connected to the inland portion of the state by four-lane U.S. 501, which runs east/west, and four-lane U.S. 17, which runs north/south. The Myrtle Beach Air Force Base also accommodates commercial aircraft.

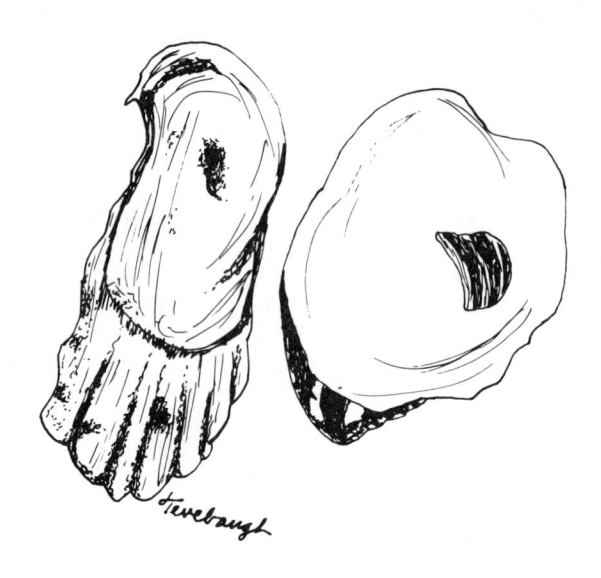

Little River

Marsh Harbour

"This may well be the most scenic golf course on the Grand Strand," said Jim Campbell, director of golf at Marsh Harbour, as he drove a golf cart along the marsh. The course also has some surprises. When you least expect it, the masts of a shrimp boat move into the fairway from behind a giant oak tree shrouded in gray moss. How did the boat get *there*? No channel is evident. But a closer look reveals inlets that snake their way through the vast marshland adjacent to Marsh Harbour fairways and greens..

Located one mile from U.S. 17, on the opposite side of S.C. 179 from Carolina Shores, a residential and recreational development, Marsh Harbour is the northernmost attraction on the South Carolina Grand Strand. Besides being perhaps the most scenic of area golf courses, it could be one of the most historic. A 600-pound granite monument in front of the clubhouse marks the spot where the Boundary House stood. The Boundary House, the oldest house recorded in Horry County, was half in North Carolina and half in South Carolina. Isaac Marion, older brother of Francis, was dining in this house in 1775 when he received word of the Battle of Lexington. This was also a favorite dueling spot. Benjamin Smith, who became a governor of North Carolina, was wounded here by a bullet in the chest.

Like the Boundary House with the state line running down the hall, Marsh Harbour is in both North Carolina and South Carolina. It draws hundreds of visitors. Although many of them come for golf, others are attracted by the beauty of the course surrounded by marsh, Intracoastal Waterway and the ocean. People from countries around the world come to photograph live oaks draped in Spanish moss, dark lagoons, huge boats of tourists and shrimp boats that move through marsh grass as silently as a mirage.

George Washington Rode Here

A mile south on U.S. 17 is the state's earliest tourist welcome center, which opened in 1967. Hospitality as well as printed

The Grand Strand

material on the history of the area is offered in the modern building. Across the highway Vereen Memorial Historical Gardens is set apart from other acreage by a split-rail fence. Visitors can walk the trail traveled by George Washington on his tour of South Carolina in 1791. This old road, the primary north-south connection in Washington's day, was the last part of the highway between Boston and Savannah to be served by stagecoach. It was isolated by swamps and rivers, and settlement developed slowly. A self-guided walk through the forest will lead to native plants that are labeled, and the old Vereen Family Cemetery beyond the end of the trail.

Toby's Old World

Toby's Old World, in the Little River business district on U.S. 17, is all that the name implies. Beyond the stained-glass door is a world of such antiques and other old things as baskets, signs, brass music stands, stuffed real native animals, turtle shells and corner cupboards filled with elegant china and crystal. There seems to be every utensil one would use in a kitchen as well as homemade pickles and sweet mustard.

Toby's Old World is proceeding carefully along a planned course that began when Toby Frye moved the main store building from its original site up the street. The smaller building, which houses sea shells, was moved to its present location nearby to make room for the huge store building. Walk out the front door of the main store, pass the gazebo, and a few feet away is a small, painted-blue church. It was once the Little River Methodist Church and was built in 1885. Today it is a restaurant.

Fish from the Hurricane!

The biggest disagreements between the people on Little River's Main Street concern which boat one should choose for deep-sea fishing. Like circus hawkers, men shout the names of the boats: "Fish from the *Hurricane!*" "Ride the *Bonita.*" "You'll pull them in on the *New Rascal.*" Little River owes its commercial success in large part to the fleet of fishing boats tied up at the Main Street harbor.

Randall-Vereen House

Of the thousands of people who go to this harbor to board fishing boats or to see the return of the boats at about 4:00 PM, few know the origin or history of the Randall-Vereen House facing the Waterway. Even in its unoccupied, dilapidated state, the wooden structure demands a glance and recognition of coastal lore. Thomas Randall, a sea captain, came here from Rochester, Massachusetts, after the War of 1812. He built three houses of similar design. One was constructed on Tilghman's Point, a privately owned tract shown on maps as Waties Island. Another of Randall's houses was built near the Waccamaw River, west of Little River; he called this one his "summer home." The two-story frame house with two large end chimneys on Main Street in Little River was later owned by a Vereen family and became known as the Randall-Vereen House. The house is not open to the public.

In the early years, businesses flourished at Little River. There were warehouses, a bank and a sawmill. When highways were constructed after the state highway system was established in 1924, the population of the village dwindled and businesses were phased out. The Randall-Vereen House is the only remnant of an age that Little River will not see again.

King Mackerel Tournament

What Mardi Gras is to New Orleans and Derby Time is to Louisville, the Arthur Smith King Mackerel Tournament is to Little River. Boats leave Little River at 8:00 AM and return at 3:30 PM on each of the two fishing days in the autumn event billed as the world's largest fishing tournament. Any boat of 18 feet in length or more can be entered for a fee of $225. Prizes totaling more than $250,000 are given to those who catch the largest king mackerel. A total of 918 boats were registered for the 1984 tournament. "I'm tickled to death," Arthur Smith said. "We've got boats here from 26 states and fishermen from 46 states and we've even got a crew here from Japan." (Steve Autry of Charlotte took top prize of $30,000 in cash and merchandise for a 38½-lb. mackerel.)

Route Traveled in Early America

From Little River, U.S. 17 leads to the beaches that form North Myrtle Beach, a union organized in 1967. The beaches (including Atlantic Beach, which is not a part of the North Myrtle Beach structure) connect with each other, and the route traveled is estimated to be the same course visitors to this coast used in colonial America.

Little River Jetties

In 1983, a $22-million jetty project, affording the only safe access from the Atlantic Ocean to the Intracoastal Waterway between Wilmington and Georgetown, was dedicated. The structure of stones projecting into the sea is about 3,600 feet on the east, and about 3,000 on the west.

Shrimp Nets. Photo by Sid Rhyne.

Cherry Grove Beach

Golf courses and restaurants line U.S. 17 from Little River to Cherry Grove Beach, the northernmost beach making up the union of North Myrtle Beach.

In the spring of 1975 when a private yacht basin was dug at Cherry Grove Beach, some clam shells, believed to date back to 1200 BC, were found. Some of them weighed five pounds and had dimensions of between six and seven inches.

This beach was named for the abundant cherry trees that grew in the area before 1860. It was first referred to as Minor's Island. On April 8, 1734, James Minor of Connecticut obtained a grant to a tract of 375 acres adjoining Little River at the junction of Cedar Creek. Title to the property was to change at least one time before it was deeded to Daniel W. Jordan in the 1840s. Jordan was a pioneer in the turpentine and tar business. He sold the property to Nicholas F. Nixon of New Bern, North Carolina, and moved to Laurel Hill, one of the plantations from which Brookgreen Gardens was made. The property was to remain in the Nixon family until some family members developed Cherry Grove Beach.

Hurricane!

In 1948 when people were looking for recreational areas in which to spend time and money, earth-moving machines, pile drivers, truck cranes and concrete mixers moved into Cherry Grove Beach. The motels and cottages constructed were still fairly new when they were jumbled into a hodgepodge of angles by Hurricane Hazel, which crashed on the coast in October, 1954. A girl in Conway was worried over the loss of a friend's house, and when it was found she shouted, "They've found Paula's house! It was only two blocks away."

Motels and cottages were rebuilt along the beach front, and, since then, dozens of prefabricated condominiums have changed the skyline at "the point" (where Cherry Grove Beach ends at the inlet) into a high-rise profile.

When construction spread into the marshes, a controversy

The Grand Strand

arose as to whether real estate should continue to boom by leveling dunes and pushing them into the swamps. In September 1977, the South Carolina Council was created by the legislature after a ten-year fight over tidelands legislation. The council dictates what can and cannot be done on the beaches and in the marshes.

World's Largest Tiger Shark

A stroll on the Cherry Grove Pier is well worth the time. The world's record tiger shark — 13 feet 10.5 inches long and weighing 1,780 pounds — was caught from this pier on June 14, 1964. Walter Maxwell, a Charlotte bricklayer, made the catch that topped the old record by 350 pounds. A shrill cry pierced the air as 1400 yards of line flew out to sea. Before the three runs made by the shark were over, 3,000 spectators had gathered to watch the contest between man and shark. The fight lasted three hours.

At the north end of the road at Cherry Grove Beach, boats go into and out of the ocean. Crabs and flounder are caught, and visitors who get up early are rewarded with a spectacular sunrise.

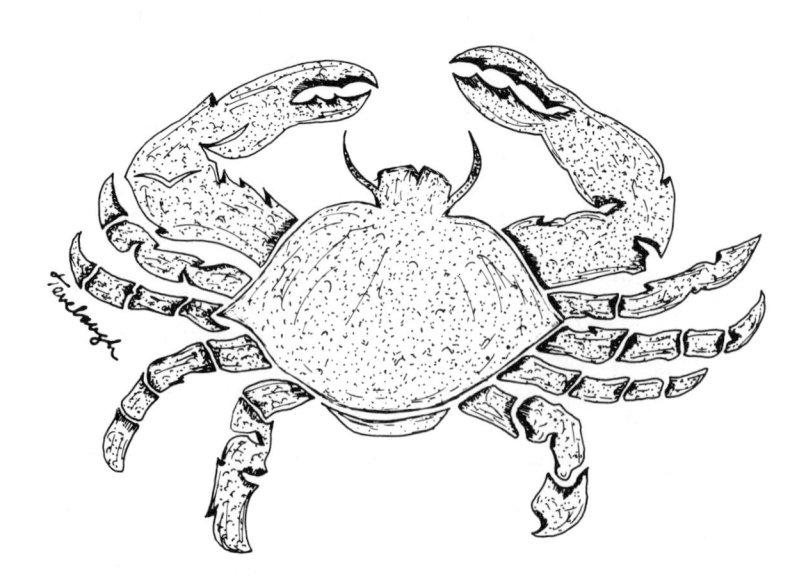

Ocean Drive Beach
Little Daytona?
Ocean Drive Beach on U.S. 17 got its name because automobile races were once held on this strand. Several years ago some Ocean Drive property owners hoped the wide and hard ocean strand would lead to Ocean Drive becoming a "little Daytona." With its natural endowments they believed this beach could rival the Florida beach, but their dream was never realized. Cars are now prohibited on the strand during summer when it is reserved for sunbathers.

Before the Revolutionary War, all the land on which this beach is situated was owned by John Bessent. Some of his descendants live in the area today. In the 1920s the first electric lights and water were installed in a home belonging to Liston H. White. The very existence of the first hotel was a source of pride, but it was a victim of Hurricane Hazel.

The Pad
During the forties, fifties and sixties, The Pad on the main drag in Ocean Drive Beach was booming with music and jam-packed with people. "The Pad was a shrine," Chris Beachley says of the dance hall that began in the 1940s as Pope's Place and later became The Pad. The people who danced the shag there do not require a definition of Beach Music. They know that when they went there to dance or just listen to the sounds of "O.D." (Ocean Drive), Beach Music was being invented.

The building that housed The Pad is still there, and some of the people who revered the hangout in its heyday refuse to believe it has faded from the scene forever. "Someone may come along, hang a sign, and The Pad will be back in business," one said.

In September 1980, hundreds of the people who had thrown nickles and dimes into the jukebox at The Pad during their teen years and shagged to the rhythm and blues reminiscent of sun and sand had a reunion at Ocean Drive Beach. Motel rooms were reserved weeks in advance of the reunion, and residents

The Grand Strand

of North Myrtle Beach received telephone calls from friends who needed rooms, but were unable to get reservations at motels that were earmarked as "headquarters" for the assemblage.

Amusement Park

The Amusement Park at Ocean Drive Beach features Mt. Olympus, a tall, fast, safe and lively water-slide.

Cruise the Intracoastal Waterway

The Intracoastal Waterway, marshes and woodlands can seldom be viewed more romantically than from the decks of The Party Ship *America*, which leaves Vereen's Marina, across U.S. 17 from Ocean Drive Beach. Passengers dine on a sumptuous buffet as the *America* winds through isolated waterways. For the Sunset Dinner Cruise, the ship advertised as the world's largest catamaran departs at 5:00 PM. It returns to Vereen's Marina and leaves again at 9:00 PM for the Moonlite Dance Cruise.

Crescent Beach

Before the development of Crescent Beach, named for the crescent-shaped arc of Long Bay, this part of the Grand Strand was used for farming. A field of corn called "the swamp field" was located where Crescent Beach is today. Because the corn was mostly free of weevils, farmers assumed that any corn grown in close proximity to salt water would be sound. Whether this assumption is correct has not been verified by agricultural research.

The Gift

According to narratives on file at the Library of Congress, there was a strong belief in this section of the county that certain people were endowed with the gift of stopping a flow of blood. One day a man was plowing a field when his mule stumbled on the lower end of a tree. The stump pierced the mule's side, and blood flowed profusely from the wound.

The plowman sent for a man who said he could stop a flow of blood. When the practitioner arrived, he looked at the wound and recited a verse. "He just squatted down and looked at the critter and said the verse three times," the plowman said. "And in no time the flow of blood stopped. It stopped just like it had been turned off."

Others in the community learned the verse and they, too, were called on to stop a flow of blood. One of them explained how the gift worked.

> "I found myself repeatin' that Bible verse over and over. Now I didn't have too much confidence in that verse, but one day we were fifteen miles up the coast and more miles than that from a doctor. We were cuttin' down a tree, and the saw went right through the pulse of a man's arm. Blood shot out just like you stuck a hog. While I repeated the verse over and over,

The Grand Strand

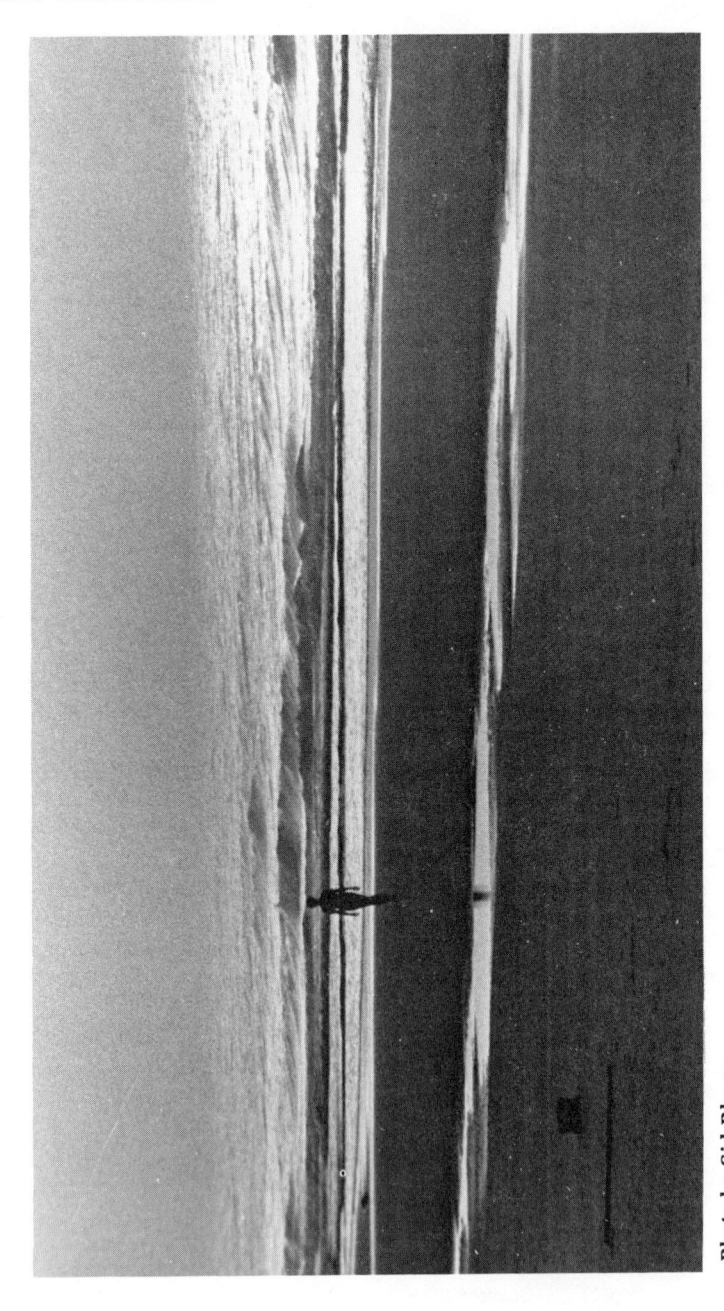

Photo by Sid Rhyne.

some other men shaved bark off a tree and pasted the shaved-up bark over the cut. That verse sure stopped the flow of blood. Now I can tell you what the verse is, but it'll only stop blood if certain ones say it. I've got that verse marked. It's the sixteenth chapter of Ezekiel, the sixth verse.

"And when I passed by thee, and saw thee polluted in thine own blood, I said unto thee *when thou wast* in thy blood, Live; yea, I said unto thee *when thou wast* in thy blood, Live." [Ezekiel 16:6, King James Version]

Development of Crescent Beach

Crescent Beach properties were formerly owned by the Bells, Wards and Lewises, well-known coastal families. But credit for developing this beach into one of the popular beaches in the union of North Myrtle Beach goes to J. W. Perrin and I. C. Jordan. Perrin was the first mayor of the town and owned large tracts of property, which were subsequently developed by others; Jordan served on the city council and incorporated Crescent Beach Corporation.

Ask almost anyone in the Crescent Beach area a question relating to the history of this place and you will be referred to C. B. Berry. He is another who played an important role in the development of Crescent Beach. Berry, who lives in Crescent Beach with his family, is a surveyor, historian and writer. He served two terms as mayor of Crescent Beach, 1956 to 1958 and 1966 to 1968. His articles appear in many publications.

A World War II airstrip located in the Crescent Beach section served the county as an airport for about thirty years. The runways at Myrtle Beach Air Force Base now accommodate most of the Grand Strand air traffic.

The Grand Strand

Haul seining. Photo by Sid Rhyne.

Atlantic Beach

In 1933 R. V. Ward sold Atlantic Beach to developer George Tyson, who named it Pearl Beach. Difficulties of the Great Depression and later the war resulted in the formation of The Atlantic Beach Company. This firm set aside a part of the oceanfront for use by the nonwhite community, and today 98 percent of the 350 year-round residents are black. Atlantic Beach chose not to be among the four towns that make up the union of North Myrtle Beach. Atlantic Beach has its own mayor, city council and chief of police. The charter of incorporation was granted on June 30, 1966.

Ethnic Pride

Cleveland Stevens, a former mayor, said he believes if the residents work hard they can enhance what they already have and can create something that is unique on the Grand Strand, something akin to Bourbon Street in New Orleans.

The Atlantic Beach Civic Center features Sand Dollar Squares, dancers who meet each Monday during summer at 7:30 PM. The 35-year-old Manhattan Guest House as well as Gore's Motel are Atlantic Beach landmarks.

Haul Seining

In the fall, Atlantic Beach is mobbed by visitors who come to see Atlantic Beachers stretch nets in the breakers and pull in varieties of fish. Sometimes fish are deep fried in a black pot over a fire in the dunes. Sea gulls also enjoy the haul seining process; they eat what remains on the strand after nets have been pulled back into the sea.

The Grand Strand

Photo by Sid Rhyne.

Windy Hill Beach

During the colonial period there was little activity along what we now know as the Grand Strand. Most of the population lived in dwellings clustered in settlements at Little River and along the Waccamaw and Pee Dee rivers. But some attention was paid to swashes (inlets) along the coast, and we know that the Gause family resided at Windy Hill Beach near the swash at Forty-eighth Avenue South. The channel was named Gause Swash, a name that was later corrupted to Goss Swash. During this century, the name was changed to White Point Swash.

William Gause came to Horry County to buy land as a result of the liberal land offer from the King of England after the king obtained it from the Lords Proprietors in July 1729. Gause took a grant to 250 acres on the swash and became keeper of an inn known for good food and hospitality.

"My! What a windy hill!"

Legend has it that President George Washington asked a Major Jackson to recommend the best accommodations along the coast when Washington was traveling through here in 1791. The major recommended Gause's place. As the president paused on a hill to catch his breath, a gust of wind almost caused him to lose his balance. "My! What a windy hill!" he said. From that day to this, Windy Hill has been the name of this town.

Like all other beaches in this area, Windy Hill sustained drastic damage from Hurricane Hazel. And like the other beaches, this one was rebuilt.

Two piers, Windy Hill Pier and Kits Pier, were among the most popular on the Grand Strand. In March 1978, the Windy Hill Pier was closed to the public when the oceanfront property was bought for a condominium complex, Ocean Pier Condominiums. Kits Pier has been closed to the public due to the construction of a condominium complex.

White Point Swash at Forty-eighth Avenue South between Kits Pier and U.S. 17 is a place of wild, natural beauty and also a prime place for shrimping and crabbing. Marsh grass (*Spar-*

The Grand Strand

tina) and plankton (drifting organisms in a body of water) produce organic food for life in the inlet.

Golf Hill

Golf Hill Executive Par 3, the only lighted Par 3 Course on the Grand Strand, is located on U.S. 17 in Windy Hill. Nine holes, 87-205 yards. Free use of 2 clubs and putter. Another place that attracts hundreds of people on a summer day is the Water Boggan on U.S. 17, north of Golf Hill.

Village of the Barefoot Traders

Village of the Barefoot Traders is a complex of shops on the side of U.S. 17 opposite the beach area. Meticulous design coupled with extreme concern for the coastal ecology have resulted in a setting with a wildlife ambience. Each of the buildings is different in design and houses a different kind of merchandise. They are clustered near a lake that is a near-perfect example of South Carolina low country flora and fauna. Tall cypress trees surround and extend into the water. An alligator now and then pulls himself to a marsh bank, and ducks sit atop old pilings.

Enter the pastel colored buildings for a complete choice of gifts as well as practical items. A shell shop has everything a collector would desire, and if you have a yen for a kitchen gadget, such as a knife designed to slice tomatoes or one to remove strawberry stems, see Tootie Allen at The Sunshine Shop.

Grand Strand Airport

A World War II airstrip located in the Windy Hill section served the county as the major airport for about thirty years. Although it is still in use, the runways at Myrtle Beach Air Force Base now accommodate much of the Grand Strand air traffic.

Meher Spiritual Center

The Meher Spiritual Center, south of Windy Hill Beach, provides a very special type of experience in a secluded area that stretches from U.S. 17 to the sea. A narrow dirt road begins at a mailbox by the highway and winds through a virgin forest of hardwoods. Nearer the sea, wood cabins come into view. They are situated among cedars, pines and live oaks draped in Spanish moss. The cabins are available to the people who come from all parts of the world to learn more of the life and the work of Meher Baba. The very name means compassionate father.

Elizabeth Patterson's Role

For an extended period of time, the late Elizabeth Patterson, as a disciple of the spiritual leader, lived in India where Meher Baba established a spiritual colony which provided a free hospital and shelters for the poor. In 1943 Patterson visited her father, Simeon B. Chapin, at his home in Myrtle Beach. She had been here before and had seen the land destined to become a spiritual center, but she rediscovered it as a perfect meeting of the directives of Meher Baba. He had decreed that any site for such a center be virgin land with more than ample water. Also, it must have good soil and a moderate climate. But more importantly, the land must be "given from the heart." Chapin was able to acquire the land, and he gave it "from the heart" to his daughter. "Everything at this center was and is given with love," Patterson said. Meher Baba visited the center three times, but, interestingly, before his first visit he directed Patterson to build his house on a certain knoll. The house sits on the highest point of the land and has a view of a lake and the sea. "Of all the sites here, he chose the best," Mrs. Patterson said.

Purpose of the Center

The spiritual leader died in January 1969, but his life of love, purity and service lives on as inspiration to those who study his words at the center near Myrtle Beach. The charter calls for use of the center for meditation, prayer, rest and renewal of the

The Grand Strand

spiritual life.

The Meher Spiritual Center is a nonprofit organization as well as a South Carolina Wildlife Sanctuary. Half of the 500-acre tract is in marshland.

The Intracoastal Waterway

Traveling south on U.S. 17 through the beaches that make up North Myrtle Beach, the ocean is on the left (east), and the Intracoastal Waterway generally runs parallel with the ocean and the highway and is on the right (west). It can be seen at several locations on the highway.

The Grand Strand section of the waterway is 95.5 miles long, 12 feet deep and 90 feet wide. Since it opened in 1936, it has supported a considerable volume of commercial shipping, principally barge traffic moving in interstate commerce. But it is also heavily used by pleasure craft of all types. Hundreds of white yachts travel this route on their migrations following the sun.

George Washington Wanted Waterway

Before white settlers arrived on South Carolina soil, Indians were using a network of tidal streams, bays and sounds as a means of communication. In 1785 George Washington recognized the need for a connecting waterway and was especially desirous of such a canal in the Great Dismal Swamp area of North Carolina and Virginia. Patrick Henry organized slave labor to build a canal in 1787 when he observed the need, but it wasn't until 1828 that construction began on the Intracoastal Waterway.

This historic route through Horry and Georgetown counties was mostly marshland until the waterway was completed and drainage improved. Now the land bordering this channel is used for farming, residential developments and golf courses. Golfers playing the Waterway Hills course on the western side of the waterway ride across the channel on a chair lift.

Waterway Hills is the only course in the world that can be reached by a tram, and the ride across the Intracoastal Waterway takes about enough time for golfers to change their regular shoes to their golf shoes.

The Grand Strand

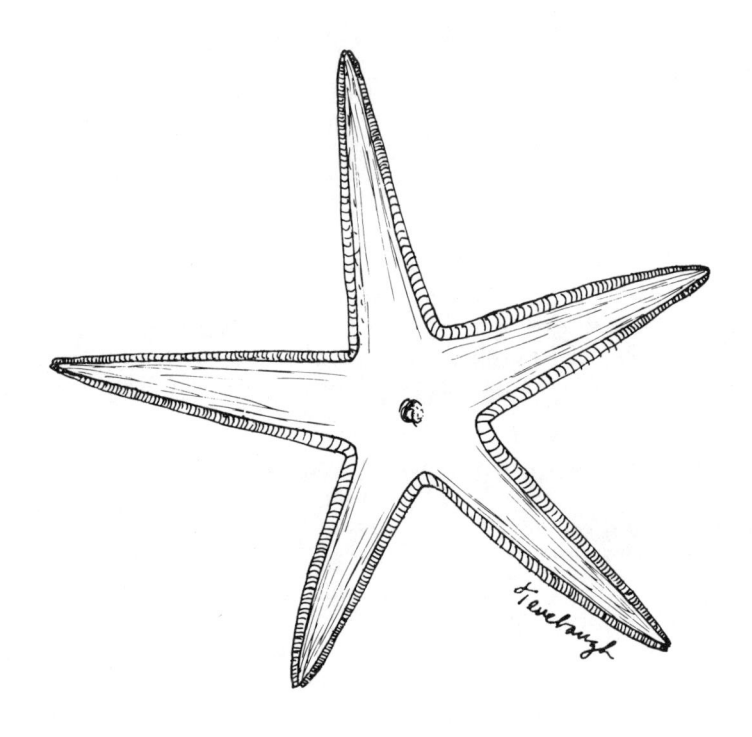

Singletons Swash

To view Singletons Swash is to have an opportunity for sightseeing that might lure you from the car. Turn toward the ocean on Lake Arrowhead Road and proceed to Shore Road, a street near the ocean that is lined on each side with condominium complexes. At the end of Shore Road, Singletons Swash flows from the ocean into the Dunes Golf and Beach Club property.

The first notice of this swash came in George Washington's diary: "Mr. Jeremiah Vareen piloted us across the Swash (which at high water is impassable, and at times, by the shifting of the Sands is dangerous) on the long Beach of the ocean, and it being a proper time of the tide we passed along it with ease and celerity to the place of quitting it . . ."

A Salt Works

During the Civil War, salt was manufactured by this swash in what was called a salt works. More than 30 buildings made up the Singletons Swash salt-making operation. Warehouses contained some 2000 bushels of salt. The works also included a horse-operated mechanical lift that pumped sea water from the swash to a storage tank with a capacity of 200,000 gallons. Despite precautions taken earlier, Yankee mariners destroyed the factory in April 1864. Recent excavations revealed ceramic grinding balls whose presence indicates that there also may have been a gunpowder factory for Confederate forces at this place.

Myrtle Beach's First Campground

Singletons Swash was the first camping site for vacationers at Myrtle Beach. Upon arrival, the first order of business was to get a supply of fresh water from a residence not too far away.

Men slept in wagons or sometimes on the sand. Women and children bedded down on mattresses brought from home. Men and boys fished by dropping lines into the surf or seines into the swash. As the sun went down, the aroma of fish frying on an

The Grand Strand

open fire rose among the pines. Women and daughters spent their time washing clothes in salt water and spreading them in the sun to bleach. They also salted down fish for winter use.

The Horry Herald carried this item on February 20, 1908:

> On last Friday quite a crowd went down to Singletons Swash to take a view of the ocean. The day was spent with pleasure, roasting and eating oysters, playing on the hills, walking on the strand and gathering sea shells washed out by the billows. After spending several hours of enjoyment, the party returned home very much satisfied over their trip.

The site of the large salt-water storage tank used in the salt works is near the eleventh fairway of Dunes Golf and Beach Club. Brick foundations for salt boiler evaporator pans are along the banks of the inlet on the Dunes Golf Club side of the channel.

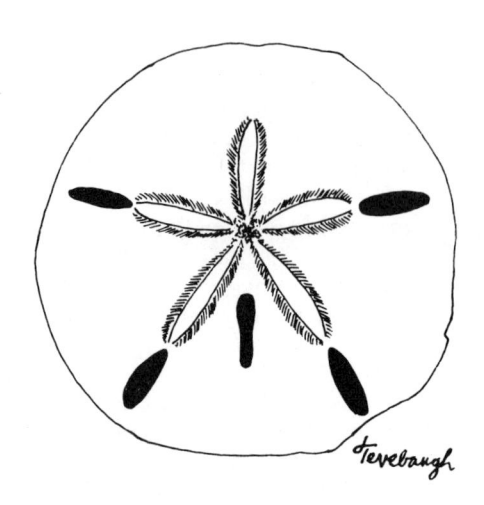

Myrtle Beach

Because there are no shipping lanes on this part of the coast, the ocean at Myrtle Beach has always been clean and pure. The first people who came here to swim were ill and came for the restorative value of the clean salt water. But before the turn of this century, there was an interest in "sea bathing" for recreation. The following article appeared in the *Georgetown Semi-Weekly Times* on August 21, 1895:

> "The season when the seaside will be the resort of most who are not absolutely indigent is within measurable distance. It is interesting to note in this connection that sea bathing had its origin in England before 1750 when Dr. Richard Russell published his treatise on the virtues of sea water. The healing virtues of the sea bath were not understood, nor was the practice of sea bathing generally resorted to. There seems to have existed a horror of the sea; indeed in medieval times a compulsory dip in its waters was a sentence often passed on the public offender. In the earlier decades of last century, Europe suffered heavily under "King's evil," the popular name for that tuberculosis affection which scourged all classes from peer to peasant. Dr. Russell, a Sussex practitioner, had observed that dwellers on the coast used to drink the sea water, bathe in it, even wash their sores in it, and bound them up with seaweed. Having satisfied himself as to the efficacy of the practise he began to prescribe it for his patients with most satisfactory results. His treatise resulted in our coast becoming largely patronized by the ailing. . . ."

The Grand Strand

Myrtle Beach's First Bathhouse

As more and more visitors came to this coast to swim, it became apparent that there would have to be some apparatus with which they could rinse themselves. Myrtle Beach's first bathhouse was in operation around the turn of the century, and Bob Montgomery kept the barrels pumped full of sun-warmed water. The people who stood under the nozzles made of perforated tomato cans luxuriated in the warm showers and were in no hurry to leave. "There are tricks in all trades," Montgomery said as he pumped cold water into the barrels. Customers jumped away from the showers when the cold water hit them.

Swimsuits were furnished by the manager of the bathhouse, six for men and six for women. When asked whether the ladies wore corsets under their long suits, the manager said he knew they did because wet corsets were hung on a line to dry along with the swimsuits.

A Name for the Village

A contest was held in 1900 to choose a name for the village on the beach. It had been generally referred to as New Town, and Conway was called Old Town. Adeline Cooper Burroughs submitted the name *Myrtle Beach* due to the abundance of myrtle bushes, and New Town was officially named Myrtle Beach.

The First Hotel

The first hotel, Seaside Inn, opened on May 23, 1901. Rates were two dollars per day for a room and three meals. Although the hotel had no plumbing and electricity, it was a good example of a well-kept country inn. Day after day luncheon and dinner menus featured such native regional dishes as fish from the sea.

By 1905 oceanfront lots had been surveyed and were selling for $25 each. However, one could obtain a lot free by promising to build on the property a house costing $500 or more. Oceanfront homes in 1909 belonged to A. W. Barrett, C. J. Epps and W. A. Freeman, all of Conway. The wooden houses had large porches with overhanging roofs that protected from the sun.

Simeon B. Chapin's Legacies

The late Simeon B. Chapin was hunting on a tract of land near today's North Myrtle Beach in 1911. The man who had

Myrtle Beach

Photo by Sid Rhyne.

The Grand Strand

been born in Wisconsin brought with him incomparable gifts: wisdom in foreseeing future development, concern for the future of the land, and wealth. Chapin, along with Burroughs & Collins Co. of Conway, established Myrtle Beach Farms Company in 1912. The company began development of Myrtle Beach. Chapin's name lives on in The Chapin Foundation of Myrtle Beach and the Chapin Memorial Library.

The Arcady Dream

In 1926, the population of Myrtle Beach was 200. John T. Woodside, a Greenville textile industrialist, along with three of his brothers bought 66,000 acres of land for $850,000. The Woodsides' dream was to create a resort where social leaders and corporate giants could enjoy the best recreation money could buy. They took the idea to Raymond M. Hood, a Rhode Island architect. Hood had assisted in the design of the Tribune Tower Building in Chicago, which had won an international contest for best design. Hood's plans for buildings in the Myrtle Beach complex included a castlelike structure overflowing with terraces and balconies. Other buildings that were to be similar in design to the Castle of Terraces and were to highlight the open, airy feeling of the beach were an open air theatre, golf house and beach club near a golf course. The name for this retreat for the rich would be *Arcady*, the very name being reminiscent of a section of ancient Greece in which peace and contentment were found in undisturbed natural surroundings. The plans for Arcady never got off the drawing boards. The economic collapse and the Great Depression prevented the proposed resort from becoming the pride of the South's Old Guard. However, the Ocean Forest Hotel and the adjoining golf club (Pine Lakes International Country Club), which were built by the Woodsides and Colonel Holmes B. Springs, were completed.

Ocean Forest Hotel

The million-dollar Ocean Forest Hotel with a wedding cake tower welled guests' eyes with wonder. For something so magnificent, with Grecian columns, Italian marble and Czechoslovakian crystal, to have risen in the sand dunes seemed a miracle. People from faraway places came to the Ocean Forest.

During the 1930s, Dorothy Knox, a reporter with the *Charlotte*

Myrtle Beach

News, was sent to Myrtle Beach to get "something of interest." She was a guest at the Ocean Forest and used the hotel as the subject for her newspaper column. Many years later she wrote a letter to the *Charlotte Observer* in which she explained why her story on the Ocean Forest was never published:

> "... However, my best "column of interest" never saw print. At that time professional gamblers from Cuba were running a casino in the tower of the Ocean Forest. You wanted a game and you got it — everything from roulette to poker. Costumes of the exhilarated mob ranged from bathing suits to ball gowns. Even though it was the Depression, money was piled on the tables like autumn leaves. I really went to town on that column, but was sick at heart not to see it in print. The men on the *News* loved it and kindly explained they couldn't spare me for a material witness had it appeared in the *News* and the joint was raided."

Myrtle Beach was incorporated in 1938. There were a few telephones in cottages on the strand, and a volunteer group operated a fire truck. But rumors of war worried the coastal residents.

Myrtle Beach Blacked Out

When the rumors became reality, all beaches on the Grand Strand were patrolled by the Coast Guard. "We saw a lot of strange lights [on the horizon] and we knew they were explosions," lumberman E. Craig Wall, Sr., remembers. "Wreckage washed up on the beach, and people living on the oceanfront were ordered to 'black out' their windows."

Spies

An article in *The Horry Herald* on April 9, 1942, said that spies had arrived by rubber boats and that cigarette smoking outside a building after dark was prohibited. Beach residents obeyed the warnings and were suspicious of strangers in the vicinity. Prisoners of war were held in custody near the coast, and some of them were allowed to work outside the camps. "I employed through the government both German and Italian

The Grand Strand

prisoners of war," Wall says. "We didn't have labor to cut pulpwood, and I thought they were pretty fair workers." After the dark and dreary days finally came to an end and the war was over, two of the prisoners who had worked for Wall became American citizens.

Count Basie, Woody Herman and Guy Lombardo

Popularity of Myrtle Beach soared after the war. Youngsters' eyes sparkled as they danced to the ragtime of Count Basie, Woody Herman and Guy Lombardo on the Marine Patio of the Ocean Forest Hotel. In 1949 *The* pavilion (there are several pavilions on the Grand Strand, but only one is *The* pavilion) was built on Ocean Boulevard at Ninth Avenue in Myrtle Beach. The young people had a new place to dance. And they had a new style of music and a new dance.

The Shag

Beginning in the late 1940s, the spirit of Myrtle Beach found one of its most vivid expressions in its music. Such vocal groups as the Ink Spots and the Mills Brothers embellished songs with jazz and swing. The songs awakened memories of the pathos and rhythm in the music of coastal plantation slaves. As the music became the vogue, it became more stagy. Generally, the tones were dominated by saxophone.

Along with changes in music, the dipping and jitterbugging that had monopolized Myrtle Beach dance floors also smoothed into a newer dance called the *shag*. This became the traditional dance to Beach Music. Feet in Bass Weejuns (and no socks) flew in cadence with such songs as "Drinkin' Wine Spo-De-O-De." If anyone during these years asked, "What *is* Beach Music?" the answer invariably was, "Music you can shag to."

Beach Music was undergoing a subtle change when the 1960s arrived. Artists using trumpets to lead the tempo replaced for the most part the musicians who had used saxophones. Shag contests were held to music that had the right beat — the music of the Catalinas, Bob Collins and The Fabulous Five and other musical groups.

Hurricane Hazel

On October 15, 1954, Hurricane Hazel crashed on Myrtle Beach and left it in shambles. Dozens of houses were totally destroyed; others were picked up and moved a block or more

Myrtle Beach

Photo courtesy of South Carolina Department of Parks, Recreation & Tourism.

The Grand Strand

away. Signs were down. Trees uprooted. The hurricane struck the beach in the morning, and before noon the sun was out and a cleanup had begun. Myrtle Beach was rebuilt, and more tourists than ever came to the Grand Strand.

Golf Boom

The golf boom began in the mid-sixties with the opening of six new courses. Even with the new courses in play, there were more golfers than tee-off times. Other courses were quickly designed and built. With the possible exception of Fort Lauderdale, Myrtle Beach experienced a more rapid growth in golfing than any other region in the nation. Jimmy D'Angelo resigned as pro at The Dunes to become administrator of Golf Holiday — a firm tying together the interests of golf and motels. D'Angelo says the phenomenal growth of Myrtle Beach golf resulted from the "golf package," which linked golfing and motels. The concept of offering a golf-lodging-meals package was envisioned by George Miller "Buster" Bryan, who built the glamorous Caravelle Motel on North Ocean Boulevard in Myrtle Beach. Bryan's idea to develop the Grand Strand into a veritable seventh heaven for golfers caught on; merchants, bankers, golf clubs, and even the brass at city council and the chamber of commerce played roles in creating Bryan's vision. The golf package has figured importantly in the development of the Grand Strand in recent years. A golf package consists of motel room, greens fee, breakfast; the motels arrange tee-off times for guests. Guests at any of the golf-oriented motels will tell you that golf made winter commercialism in Myrtle Beach possible. In late winter and early spring, more golfers are playing the Grand Strand's courses than are playing in any other resort in the world.

Golf courses are everywhere on the Grand Strand. But while golfing is truly the most sociable sport here, it is not the only one. Tennis may never equal the rank of golf here, but racquet clubs have been built near the waterway and the ocean, and some motels offer tennis in their golf package.

A New Life-Style

A new life-style developed with the coming of the golfers. Entrepreneurs built condominiums facing golf course greens and fairways. It has been rumored that some property owners actually gave away property for golf courses in order to develop the surrounding acreage. The condominium craze spread rapidly; condos are rising now on almost any available spot of land near the ocean or golf courses.

In September 1974, the Ocean Forest Hotel, which had changed hands at least nine times, was razed. Today Ocean Forest Villas are on the property. The pavilion has been enlarged, and there are 25 rides and other attractions in the amusement park at the pavilion.

The Carousel

Imagine one of the world's few carousels with ponies, lions, frogs, llamas, zebras, giraffes and sea monsters carved by Bavarian woodcarvers, sliding up, then down. And all of this to the tempo of the magic music of a Wurlitzer 165-band organ reminiscent of the Roaring Twenties. The 32-ton carousel at the Myrtle Beach Pavilion was brought here in the 1950s, and the organ, which was later added, still plays some of the original music rolls.

The Ultimate Organ

An organ of almost mystical reputation is the band organ built by A. Ruth & Sohn of Germany. The organ offers concerts to standing-room-only crowds from June through Labor Day and is rich in inspiration and history. After the instrument was featured at the World Exposition in 1900, it was returned to Germany where a team of six horses pulled the treasure from village to village where people gathered to listen and dance. Some years after that, the instrument was brought to a home on the island of Martha's Vineyard, and in 1954 it was sold to Myrtle Beach Farms Company for display at the pavilion. The organ has 400 pipes and 98 keys, and one of its most identifiable features is its front where 18 figures catch the eye as 12 of them move in rhythm with the music. Some original music sheets are still used. Many people come to see the organ just to appreciate the workmanship of the cabinet.

Convention Center

The Myrtle Beach Convention Center was built in 1970 at Twenty-first Avenue and Oak Street and then expanded to over 55,000 square feet as Myrtle Beach grew in popularity as a place to have conventions. The auditorium can serve as a 14,000-square-foot exhibit hall. The South Carolina Hall of Fame, honoring those contemporary and past citizens who have made outstanding contributions to South Carolina's heritage, is located in the civic alcove of the Convention Center.

The Grand Strand

Variety in Shopping

Everything in the world has been done to make Myrtle Beach stores attractive and have them offer fashions, jewelry and other merchandise gratifying tourists' every yen. Sixty-seven businesses at Myrtle Square Mall on U.S. 17 whet shopping appetites, and boutiques at Rainbow Harbor north of the mall impress sophisticated, international travelers. The Hidden Village features gifts, cross-stitch, crafts, confectionery, soaps and linen, among other things. This shopping area is tucked behind an antique shop in the Restaurant Row section of U.S. 17 north of downtown Myrtle Beach.

The Nation's Largest Gift Shop

The Gay Dolphin Gift Shop began in 1944 on the boardwalk at 910 North Ocean Boulevard in a building about half the size of a mobile home. It is in the same location today, but has been expanded to include the three-story building extending from the boardwalk to the ocean, a building across the street facing Ocean Boulevard, and the Straw Cove building on the third row. Besides that, two huge warehouses are off premises. About 8000 customers visit the Gay Dolphin on a summer day. Justin Plyler, owner, says, "We advertise as the nation's largest gift shop on the basis of the total square footage, on which we are only slightly larger than our nearest competitor, and also on the basis of the number of items carried—and this is nearly three times the number of items carried by our nearest competition." Over 60,000 different items are available in the Gay Dolphin.

Restaurant Row

Regional cuisine is seldom as delectable as on Restaurant Row, where restaurants line U.S. 17 between Myrtle Beach and Windy Hill. Diners can choose from Cagney's Old Place, Gullyfield, and Slug's Rib, and you can also browse through thousands of books at the Book Shoppe, across U.S. 17 from Cape Craftsman.

Nightlife

For those seeking nightlife, the culmination of the dream may be a lounge in one of the motels, such as the Hojo Lounge at Howard Johnson's Resort Inn on Shore Drive, eight miles north of Myrtle Beach. The fabulous Myrtle Beach Hilton (take Chestnut Road from U.S. 17 nine miles north of Myrtle Beach at Hawaiian Village) has rooftop disco. The Ocean Dunes at 74th Street North and the nearby Sand Dunes offer live entertainment. One cannot go wrong at the Sheraton at 71st Avenue North or the Turtle Lounge and Captain's Bridge in the Yachtsman complex on 14th Avenue. The Coquina Club at the Landmark on Ocean Boulevard at 15th Avenue South is another favorite.

"John Belk's Place"

John M. Belk, a former mayor of the city of Charlotte and chairman of the board of Belk Stores Services, built the striking St. John's Inn. The motel stands at North Ocean Boulevard and Sixty-ninth Street in Myrtle Beach. St. John's Inn is famous for its restaurant, which features prime rib. It is also noted for having one of the most eye-catching signs on the Grand Strand. The round emblem features the name, St. John's Inn, encircled by two sea horses. But for the most part, visitors say they have reservations at "John Belk's Place," rather than St. John's Inn, as Belk is well-known in the nation.

Grand Strand's Contribution to Twentieth Century Music

Although 30 years have passed since the concept of Beach Music began, it is still the entertainment king of the strand. Radio stations devote whole programs to it and record shops around the Carolinas report phenomenal sales. Such artists as Maurice Williams and The Chairman of the Board made Beach Music recordings at the Arthur Smith Recording Studio in Charlotte in 1980. The recordings included "Forever Beach" and "Carolina Girls." Beach Music is undoubtedly the Grand Strand's contribution to twentieth century music.

Waccamaw Pottery

Waccamaw Pottery, located on U.S. 501, near the bridge that spans the Intracoastal Waterway, has grown into a shopping complex of such proportions that it is now an important Grand Strand attraction. At the Pottery, one can see silk and dried floral demonstrations and glass cutter exhibits. Located next to Waccamaw Pottery is a 46-store Outlet Park.

A Whale Large Enough to Have Swallowed Jonah

South of the Swamp Fox roller coaster on Ocean Boulevard in Myrtle Beach is a place that was once named Hurl Rock Beach. In 1900 word spread through this quiet place that a whale large enough to have swallowed Jonah had washed ashore. When

The Grand Strand

news of the beached whale was dispatched to Conway, people made plans to go to Myrtle Beach and see the wonder that had washed up. They rode a ferry across the Waccamaw River, then boarded the little train Black Maria for the remainder of the trip. The travelers sat on boards placed by the sides of the flat cars. They held umbrellas as protection from engine sparks, but even then holes were burned in some of the umbrellas and several garments caught fire. The train stopped at Pine Island where the people, some carrying picnic baskets, boarded wagons for a ride across the dunes.

Those who viewed the harpooned whale were all but overcome with surprise. Frank Burroughs, a tall man, stood beside the whale and held a hoe as high as he could, and the hoe did not reach the top of the mammal.

A group of whalers arrived to claim their treasure. They explained that after they had harpooned the whale they had been forced to cut the rope quickly when a storm blew up. (The process from harpooning to the death of the whale could have taken a day or longer. The tight curb on whaling today was not in existence at that time when there was a demand for whalebone to be used as stays in women's corsets, ribs in umbrellas, and whale oil was used for lamps and candles.) The harpooners cut the meat from the bones and left with their bounty, leaving most of the skeleton of the whale on the sand. Children played in the skeleton.

Myrtle Beach State Park

Myrtle Beach State Park, on the eastern side of U.S. 17 at the southern tip of Myrtle Beach, was constructed by the Civilian Conservation Corps during the administration of President Franklin D. Roosevelt. This is the most visited of any of the state parks, and the terrain in this part of the Low Country is as rugged and as gentle as the lowcountrymen it has bred.

The camping area of the park was laid out on wooded tracts so as to leave all the shade possible. The best trees are still there, and a natural look was retained. Signs show the way to picnic tables, the outdoor swimming pool and the 720-foot saltwater fishing pier.

The popular Sculptured Oak Nature Trail starts from the forest of loblolly pines and goes to a stream where one is likely to see animal tracks, if not the animals. Passing by magnolias, the trail continues through a forest of hickory trees, then yaupon hollies, and ends in the dunes.

Camping under the oaks here is a favorite pastime of thousands, and cabins are available year-round for the same rates as summer rental rates.

If you are not camping, as the dinner hour approaches and campers fire their outdoor grills, spread a picnic meal on a table and enjoy the breeze whipping off the ocean.

The Grand Strand

Black Panther by Anna Hyatt Huntington. Photo by Sid Rhyne.

Myrtle Beach Air Force Base

Two lizard-green A-10 aircraft rise over the pines. They turn in formation over Myrtle Beach Air Force Base, then head toward the ocean. Nicknamed the Thunderbolt II, the A-10 single-seat twin-turbofan is the only aircraft of its type in the world. In 1977 the first one touched down at this base across U.S. 17 from Myrtle Beach State Park, and since that time this field has become sanctuary to 72 of the planes.

From June 1940 to December 1941, the airport was used by various units of the Army Air Corps. They flew air photographic and charting missions in the local area and practiced gunnery missions along the beaches of the Grand Strand. When the 112th Observation Squadron arrived early in 1941 to provide coastal defense, support for a bombing and gunnery range began. The range was designated Myrtle Beach Army Air Field on November 8, 1943, and by this time it was composed of some 100,000 acres of owned and leased land. Five air-to-ground ranges were located in the Myrtle Beach area, a demolition range and three bombing ranges were near Conway, and the Georgetown area had two bombing ranges as well as one for demolition.

Training of airmen and construction of facilities were pushed at a fast pace. While some of the men were being trained and sent to fly with Lieutenant Colonel James Doolittle in the first raid on Tokyo, 114 buildings were being built and connected by a network of roads and runways. The personnel shortage was eased now and then when draftees arrived. To aid in the crunch, men were brought from a German prisoner of war camp near Myrtle Beach and given housekeeping detail.

After World War II, the field remained active until its shutdown in 1947. The runways and tower were offered to Myrtle Beach to be used as a municipal airport.

The Department of Defense rehabilitated the site in 1953, and the first commanding officer was Colonel (later General) Robert Emmons, one of Doolittle's Raiders in the famous 1942 bombing of Japan. This station went on to assist in crises around the

The Grand Strand

world including the Lebanon, Cuban and Dominican Republic conflicts.

The Black Panther

In the mid-1950s Colonel Francis Gabreski of the 345th Tactical Fighter wing went to see Anna Hyatt Huntington at her home Atalaya, near Brookgreen Gardens. He asked her to carve a panther to be used as a symbolic mascot for his squadron. The black panther is on the insignia of the squadron, worn on the left shoulder of the flying suits. It is also displayed on aircraft used by the squadron. Mrs. Huntington had executed many of the statues in Brookgreen Gardens, which she and her husband had designed and built. At first she refused to comply with the Colonel's request, saying she was preparing to leave South Carolina for her home in New York and that, furthermore, although she had carved panthers before, all of her models had been sent away. Yet before Colonel Gabreski left her home, she agreed to carve the panther for the squadron.

Several years later when the squadron was deployed to Spain, the panther statue was taken along as mascot. When it was returned to Myrtle Beach Air Force Base, it was placed on a brick pedestal containing a time capsule. In the capsule is a roster of the pilots with the squadron at that time, a squadron insignia, and literature on prisoners of war and men missing in action. There are also photographs of the aircraft used at that time, which were the predecessors to the A-10.

The panther, now on display at the Myrtle Beach Air Force Base, is down in a fighting position with ears lowered, fangs bared and with the claws of the right front paw exposed.

Joint Military and Civilian Use

Today the field at this base serves jetcraft coming and going from the Grand Strand. Joint military and civilian use of the runways started with the formal opening of Piedmont Airlines terminal facilities on July 9, 1975. Piedmont offers four non-stop flights daily from Charlotte. Passengers traveling from other cities and states connect with the flights in Charlotte. Piedmont also offers one flight daily from Greensboro with a stop in Wilmington.

Myrtle Beach Air Force Base is open to the public on a limited basis. Anyone desiring a free tour should phone (803)

Myrtle Beach Air Force Base

238-7552 for reservations. For groups, three weeks advance notice is necessary.

Tour buses leave from the main gate. A guide calls attention to rows of A-10 fighter planes lined up on the field. They cost from eight to ten million dollars each, and they fly low over the target, about tree level. The guns in the noses are accurate up to one mile from the target. The A-10 carries the most powerful cannon of any airplane in the world. This aircraft is designed to shoot 4200 rounds of ammunition per minute, but the plane cannot carry that much. Consequently, all ammunition on board can be discharged in 20 seconds. The A-10 can reach any target in the world well within 24 hours, and although it is not the speediest, it probably is the most maneuverable plane anywhere.

Among facilities shown to tourists are dormitories, a bank, an exchange (department store), two Olympic-size pools, the NCO club, tennis courts, gym with full basketball court, automobile and woodworking hobby shop, child care center, officers' club, elementary school, duck pond for fishing, a full service (except for obstetrics/gynecology) hospital, and a chapel.

The Grand Strand

Surfside Beach

In 1920 George Holliday of Galivants Ferry purchased much of the property that is Surfside Beach, on U.S. 17 south of Myrtle Beach Air Force Base, and named it Floral Beach in honor of his wife, Flora. The name was changed to Surfside in 1950 when a group of investors bought a portion of the property.

Local Lore

The people who lived here in the 1800s depended on observations of animals and people for weather forecasts instead of on weather stations throughout the world as we do today. When they saw hogs running about and picking up sticks and trash, it meant cold weather was coming. Other indications of impending cold weather were birds fluffing their feathers and chickens hovering together late in the afternoon. A rooster crowing while standing on a fence meant fair weather was ahead; a rooster crowing while on the ground indicated rain. If a snake were killed during hot, dry weather, hanging the snakeskin belly-side-up in a tree ensured the coming of rain.

A Hard Life

People who lived in the pinelands and oak groves near this place learned the facts of life early:

> "My ma, she had a time. Here's my ma's fifth one a-comin'. Nobody for five miles and the knee-high one crawlin' over her in the bed in a fit. Havin' a fit and another one a-bornin'."

People who lived on this stretch of the coast, almost surrounded by water, had to "doctor" themselves. Few physicians were available during illness or when childbirth was imminent:

> "Never had a doctor for me yet. My mammy good granny woman. She caught two sets of twins for me — Isaac and Rebecca; David and Caneezer."

The Grand Strand

Sharks Teeth Found Here

Collectors of sharks teeth have spread the word that Surfside Beach is a prime place for locating them. They are also sold in gift shops, but if one looks closely, the shiny, three-cornered teeth can be found on the sand.

Military Retirees Settle Here

Servicemen from Myrtle Beach Air Force Base enjoy this beach and when they are given new duty stations around the world the word on Surfside Beach goes with them. Davidson College once questioned its alumni on their plans for the future and one man wrote that he began his career in the Air Force at Myrtle Beach Air Force Base and when his military career ends he plans to retire at Surfside Beach. Myrtle Beach Air Force Base is a drawing card for hundreds of military retirees who get medical care and other free or discounted services. Many military retirees have settled at Surfside Beach where they and their dependents have nearby access to government physicians and can shop at PXs and commissaries as well as enjoy friendships with other veterans and their families.

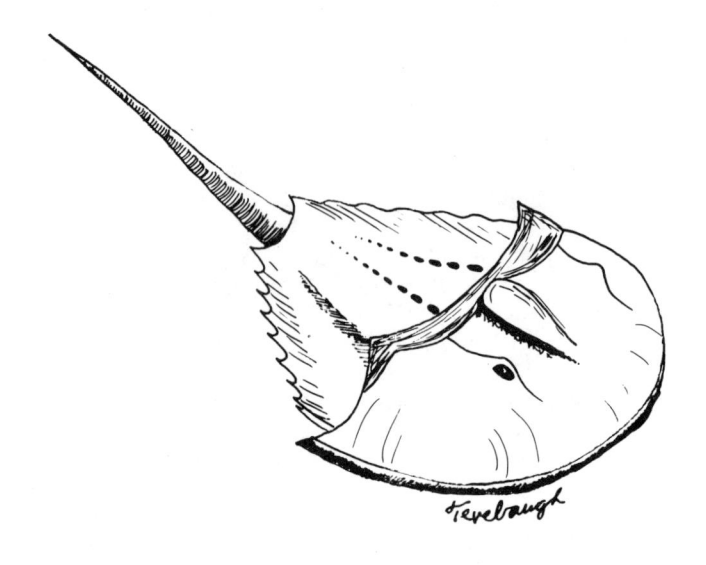

Garden City Beach

Oyster beds ... they line much of the marshland around Garden City Beach at the Horry/Georgetown County line on U.S. 17 south of Surfside Beach. Hard-as-cement oyster shells are shades of gray.

"Make my livin' with ister."

Ben Horry, born in slavery south of Garden City, made his living in his last days by roasting oysters and serving them. "Make my livin' with ister," he said. "Tide going out, I go out in a boat with the tide. Tide bring me in with sometimes ten, sometimes fifteen or twenty bushels." Ben Horry is gone now, but oysters are a favorite item at nearby Murrell's Inlet seafood restaurants, although they are not the locally-harvested variety.

Migratory Residents

With its hundreds of oceanfront and by-the-creek cottages and inland parks designated as sites for mobile homes, Garden City Beach is unique. It is not a New England village, nor is it Miami Beach. Rather, it offers a strictly South Carolina coastal way of life. So many people have become a part of this way of life and go back each year to the same cottage or mobile home that they are referred to as being migratory.

The North Jetty

Do not miss the North Jetty, a portion of the Murrells Inlet navigation project at the southern tip of Garden City Beach. The jetty was built of rocks weighing up to 200 pounds. It extends 3445 feet from the shore and has a top elevation of 9 feet above the low-water level. This jetty, completed in January 1979, contains a weir for sand bypassing at high tide. The purpose of the jetty is to stabilize the inlet across an ocean bar so commercial and recreational boats harbored in the Murrells Inlet waters can navigate the channel at all times — regardless of tides.

The fishing pier at Garden City Beach is considered by fishermen to be one of the finest on the Grand Strand.

The Grand Strand

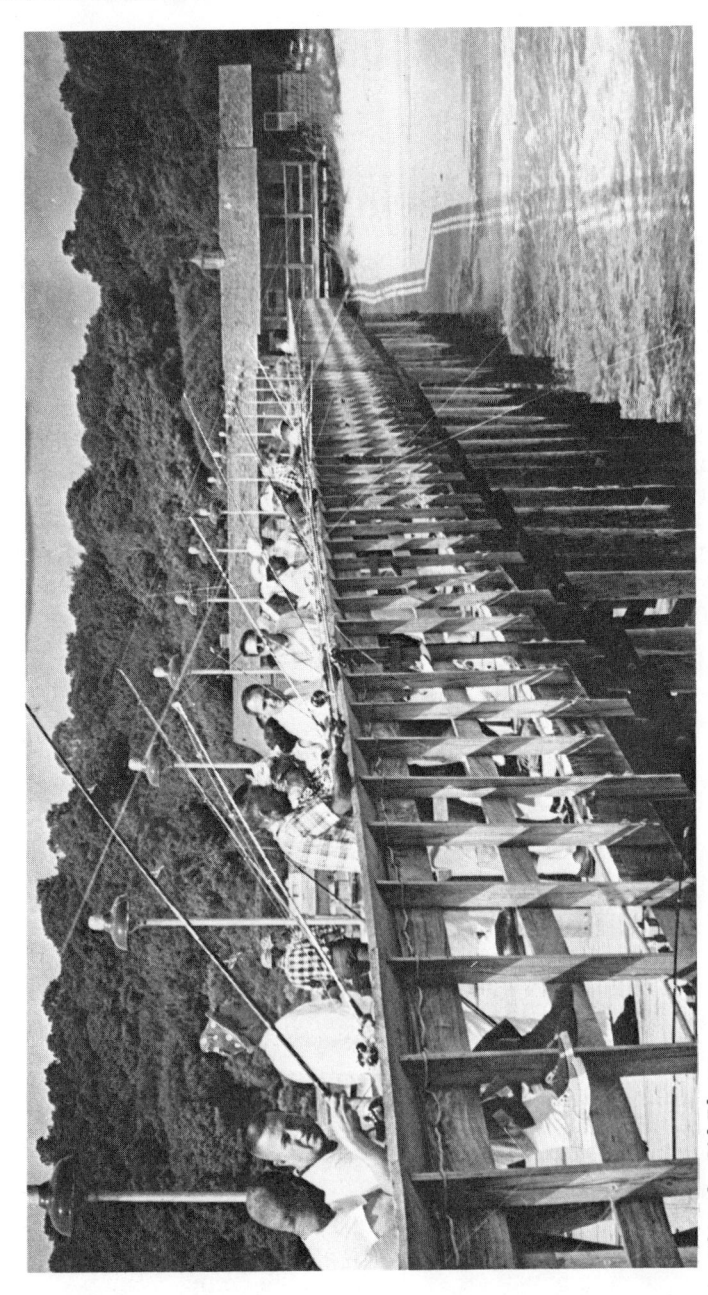

Photo by Sid Rhyne.

Murrells Inlet

"Skins! And furs!" yelled Blackbeard as he sailed under the skull and crossbones into an island off Murrells Inlet. But before the people on the island could escape to safety, the man with his hair braided was upon them flashing both a sword and pistol.

Sound like a movie or television show? Edward Teach (Blackbeard) terrorized the people on the Carolina coast between 1716 and 1717 and is believed to have buried chests of treasure at Murrells Inlet and then feasted on oysters and shrimp washed down with rum.

Oldest Fishing Village in the State

Located about ten miles south of Myrtle Beach on BUS 17, Murrells Inlet is the oldest fishing village in the state. It was named for John Morrall who purchased 610 acres on the inlet in 1731. Descendants of plantation owners still live at this place where the atmosphere today creates imagery of the days when every inch of land by the Waccamaw River was planted in rice. Wachesaw, Sunnyside and Brookgreen are some of the plantations near this inlet. Murrells Inlet was a favored place for a summer visit when the heat and mosquitoes made it nearly impossible for the planters and their families to remain on the plantations. This was also an ideal place for salt making, and Joshua John Ward of Brookgreen had a salt works at Murrells Inlet capable of making 30 or 40 bushels of salt per day. His salt works was destroyed by Federal troops during the Civil War. The enemy also shelled and set fire to schooners that were being used to ship cotton from Murrells Inlet during that war.

Woodland

Woodland, a summer residence that dated from the mid-1800s, was a Murrells Inlet landmark, but unfortunately it

The Grand Strand

Photo by Heidi Hall. Courtesy of Pawleys Island Perspective.

recently was destroyed by fire. At one time, it was owned by Dr. Edward Thomas Heriot, who planted rice on Mount Arena Plantation on Sandy Island.

The late Miss Corrie Dusenbury remembered the storm of October 13, 1893. She was a child at that time, and she lived at Woodland.

>Papa, a businessman, had gone to Georgetown that day and had left Mama in charge with the help of a hired man named Zack. When Zack came running up to Mama and said the waves had risen over the creek bank and were headed toward the house, she responded, with no emotion at all in her voice, "Place the flour barrel on the stove and all lower dresser drawers on the bed." After Zack had done this, he ran to the front door to bolt it. "Don't lock the door," Mama said quietly, "open the door so when the water reaches it, it won't break the door down." It was Mama's lack of alarm that kept the children from becoming anxious. As long as she went about and spoke with such composure, we were not afraid.
>
>Mama called to the children and informed us that we should find a place on the stairs to sit. "Take the dog with you," she said, "and don't sit on a step too near the top nor too near the bottom."
>
>As we sat there, the water came through the house toward the creek. On the water were many things bobbing up and down, including some white chickens.
>
>When the steamboat reached the landing at Wachesaw in the evening, Papa got on his mount and picked his way along the road which was blocked by fallen trees. He met someone on the road who told him we were safe, and he slowed his speed a bit but was still exhausted when he reached home.

Indian Shell Mounds

Under the large trees beside the marsh are shell mounds believed to date back to the time when Indians occupied this village. Conch shells have been found with holes in them.

The Grand Strand

These are said to have been used as hoes by Indian women. They slipped their fingers through the holes and dug the soil and planted corn.

Artists and writers have chosen to live along the inlet under the oak trees. Water-color and charcoal prints of houses by the creek, boats riding at anchor, white shore birds resting on the branches of giant oaks and other Murrells Inlet scenes can be bought at local gift shops. Mickey Spillane lives in a frame house at the end of a road by the inlet. He has written many books, but has not used Murrells Inlet as a setting for his stories. One hears his name spoken occasionally at Oliver's Lodge, a local seafood restaurant. "I typed a manuscript. Had to type all night," a cashier said. "He doesn't come in during the busy times," a waitress pointed out. "He 'back doors' it (picks up his orders at the back door)." Although tourists frequently ride by the house with the sports car (said to be a gift of the late John Wayne) in the driveway, they seldom get a glimpse of Mickey.

Waccamaw River Tours

The Island Queen II leaves from the Wacca Wache Marina at the end of S.C. 62 and the Waccamaw River near Murrells Inlet for daily tours during summer. An evening cruise featuring a stop at a Waccamaw River restaurant for dinner is also offered. *The Island Queen II* follows a historic river route by such celebrated Old South plantations as Chicora Wood, Hasty Point and Arundel. Sandy Island, whose residents have to travel by boat to come to the mainland, is a highlight of the river tours.

Charter Fishing Boats

Fleets of fishing boats leave Murrells Inlet harbor daily for the Gulf Stream. U.S. Coast Guard approved ships such as *Flying Fisher*, *Capt. Dick's* and *New Inlet Princess* have electric fishfinders, radar, ship-to-shore radiophones and air conditioning. Their crews are skilled in conducting safe trips to areas where fish are likely to be plentiful. Snapper, grouper and sea bass fishing expeditions are among the more popular.

Murrells Inlet Seafood Restaurants

It is not uncommon for Murrells Inlet restaurants to have regular customers who think nothing of making a 200-mile trip just to dig into a seafood platter. Names like Drunken Jack's, Bay

Murrells Inlet

Fishing Boats at Murrells Inlet. Photo by La'tka Thompson, courtesy of *Pawleys Island Perspective*.

The Grand Strand

Harbor, Oliver's Lodge, Sea Captain's House, Pilot House and Planters Back Porch are the likes of which have made this place nationally famous for its fare from the ocean.

Some of the restaurant cooks say they obtain seafood daily from local fishing boats. When an order is received in the kitchen, the seafood is breaded, cooked and served tongue-searing hot; no food is prepared in advance of a customer's order. The top seller is the combination seafood platter consisting of fish, oysters, scallops, shrimp and deviled crab. The second biggest seller is a platter of fried fish; shrimp rates third.

Customers can expect to stand in line to be served during summer when crowds converge on restaurants in late afternoon, but winter fans keep Murrells Inlet seafood restaurants open year-round.

Lowcountry Stores

Adjoining but very different shops are located at U.S. 17 By-pass at Murrells Inlet. A French crepe-maker or a Chinese wok set can be picked up at this place. Quilts and hand-woven bedspreads are featured, as well as original watercolor Low Country scenes painted by local artists. Stay for lunch and sample an inlet shrimp sandwich in the dining room or on the patio under a giant oak.

A Murrells Inlet restaurant. Photo by Sid Rhyne.

Brookgreen Gardens

The gargantuan gift of Brookgreen Gardens to the people through a charitable corporation made this part of the Grand Strand one of the richest, most envied spots in the country. The outdoor museum is located on U.S. 17 south of Murrells Inlet on the site of four former rice plantations.

Huntington Comes to South Carolina

In 1930 Archer Milton Huntington and his sculptor wife, Anna, were sailing to the West Indies when they stopped at Georgetown for supplies. Before they resumed their trip, Huntington had bought Brookgreen, Laurel Hill, The Oaks and Springfield — adjoining plantations. His father, Collis P. Huntington, who built the Southern Pacific Railway and ran several important steamship lines, had been one of America's 12 richest men.

Legends were affectionately told of the plantations Huntington bought. Laurel Hill had been owned by Gabriel Marion, nephew of the Revolutionary General Francis Marion. William Allston (1738-1781), who served as a captain under Francis Marion, owned Brookgreen Plantation and left it to a son, Benjamin. Under his will William Allston left to his son Washington (who later became a well-known artist) acreage called The Spring, a tract believed to be Springfield Plantation. William Allston's cousin, Joseph, owned The Oaks Plantation, which adjoined Brookgreen. This Joseph Allston left The Oaks to a namesake grandson, who married Aaron Burr's daughter Theodosia.

On December 30, 1812, Theodosia was disconsolate over the death of her 10-year-old son. She boarded a small vessel at Brookgreen and rode "down with the outgoing tide" to Georgetown where she would board *The Patriot*, a sailing vessel bound for New York. Theodosia's husband had won the governorship of South Carolina that year and was busy with political matters, but he felt that a visit with her father in New York would be a tonic to Theo in her depressed state.

The Grand Strand

Jaguar. Photo by Heidi Hall, courtesy of *Pawleys Island Perspective.*

Brookgreen Gardens

A gale was blowing in from the sea as Theodosia boarded *The Patriot*, and the talk on the wharf was that a devastating storm was raging off the coast of Nags Head. Soon after the sails of the vessel were out of sight, rumors also spread of privateers in the vicinity. *The Patriot* was never heard from again, and its fate has not been determined.

There were plantations and there were *plantations*. The ones bought by Huntington were identified with rice growing. Most of their owners had scaled the heights of early South Carolina society, and some had been members of the Winyah Indigo Society. Avenues of live oaks that once led to old homesites remained at Brookgreen and Laurel Hill.

A Sculptor's Paradise

When the Huntingtons returned from their voyage and got their ducks in a row, they set about designing Brookgreen as a setting for Mrs. Huntington's sculpture. "Mr. Huntington enjoyed advertising his wife," Genevieve Willcox Chandler, a former employee of Huntington, says. "He enjoyed publicizing her and having her considered the greatest woman sculptor." But as Anna Hyatt Huntington executed her work and the statues were moved into the garden, the Huntingtons decided to also exhibit the work of other artists. Sculpture from around the country arrived and additional display space was required. Sections of the garden were extended, fields and woodlands were cleared, and pools were built as focal points. The garden spread far beyond the famous avenue of oaks planted by the first owner of Brookgreen Plantation and the old kitchen that had been used when Joshua John Ward planted rice at this place.

Ten Million Dollars to Play With

"Mrs. Huntington was the boss [of the garden's design] and Mr. Huntington had the money," a close friend named Mosier said. "He gave her ten million to play with, to use in doing her sculpture (and creating Brookgreen Gardens)."

"Oh, he was a country gentleman," Genevieve Chandler recalls, "in his knickers, his high socks and his size-thirteen shoes, which were made in London. He rode through the garden on a fine horse and supervised the work. Wild boars ran around, and deer were also in the forest. Then he would return to his office and sit by a fire of oak wood. He was very extravagant with oak wood, as there was plenty of it."

The Grand Strand

Photo by Heidi Hall, courtesy of *Pawleys Island Perspective*.

As the work progressed, the Huntingtons became obsessed with the idea of retaining the flavor of the former rice plantation of Joshua John Ward.

The Plantation Under Ward

Ward had been born at Brookgreen in 1800 and had become the grandee of lowcountry rice planters. In 1850 he produced 3,900,000 pounds of rice, the largest yield in the district, with the help of more than 1000 slaves. Ward had a reputation of being a hard taskmaster. Some of the women who worked "in rice" for Ward said "Ol Mas' Josh" expected them to work at least one-half an acre of rice per day in whatever task was assigned to them — planting, hoeing or cutting and tying in sheaves. What's more, the women were not allowed to straighten up as they worked from the beginning of a row to the end, according to legend.

As important as labor and land in Ward's success was the discovery of a high-yield strain called big grain rice. Colonel Joshua John Ward wrote a letter on November 16, 1843, in which he said:

> "In 1838, my overseer, Mr. James C. Thompson, a very judicious planter, residing on my Brook Green estate, accidentally discovered in the barnyard during the threshing season a part of an ear of Rice, from the peculiarity of which he was induced to preserve it, until he had an interview with me."

The seed from this ear of rice was planted in 1840 and yielded 49 bushels of "clean rice." The following year the seed rice was sown in a field of 21 acres and yielded 1170 bushels.

Restoration

Although the Ward manor house was gone when the Huntingtons purchased Brookgreen, they designed the garden with the old Ward kitchen in the center. A boxwood garden that dates back to the Wards is outside the kitchen.

Huntington spread word that he was looking for a gardener who was especially gifted in collecting and planting native wild flowers. Officials at Clemson University told Huntington that if he searched the whole state of South Carolina, he could not find a man better fitted to the job than Frank G. Tarbox, Jr. Tarbox was hired, and he spent many years landscaping and

The Grand Strand

cultivating Brookgreen Gardens. He also searched the woods for native plants and was pleased with the different kinds of milkweeds and other lowcountry specimens he found. His close association and friendship with Huntington seemed to be especially pleasing to both of them.

Although the South was in the depths of the Great Depression when the Huntingtons came here, and those who were working at all were earning only pennies a day, the economy around Brookgreen took an upswing. Huntington gave jobs in the garden to some who needed work. When rumor traveled the grapevine that Huntington's income was $80,000 per day, the wealthy couple were asked time and again for financial assistance. They were sensitive to the needs around them and gave brick for a church building, flooring for the house of an employee, and a tombstone to an old man nearing his hundredth birthday. The stone was inscribed with the man's name, Welcom Beese, 1833-19. Welcom Beese died March 21, 1942. The death date is not inscribed on the stone, which is now in a graveyard administered by Faith Memorial Episcopal Church at Pawleys Island and located on U.S. 17 south of Brookgreen.

Mrs. Huntington's Masterpiece

One day as Mrs. Huntington worked in her studio at Atalaya, the Huntington home on the seashore portion of the property, she summoned Joe, an employee. Joe was asked to search the countryside for a scrawny horse that could be used as a model for a statue of Don Quixote on his exhausted mount, Rocinante. Joe returned to Atalaya with a horse that was surely dying. Its bones showed sharply under its rough coat; its heavy head hung down to its knees; foam hung from the animal's mouth.

Mrs. Huntington made a sling to hold the emaciated horse upright so it could be used as a model. She fed the animal and nursed it back to health as she worked. "She wouldn't let anyone else care for the horse," George Bessellieu, a former employee, said. "She let others clean the stable, but that was all."

The statue, which stands near the Visitor's Pavilion, won recognition as being a masterpiece of detail. Anna Hyatt Huntington's *Don Quixote* was joined in September 1971 by C. Paul Jennewein's *Sancho Panza*, a rustic companion to the old visionary.

"Mrs. Huntington was famous for her statues of horses," Genevieve Chandler recalls. "She always said she could carve anything if a horse were a part of the design."

Brookgreen Gardens

Although Huntington ran his worldwide interests from other residences, it is believed he thoroughly enjoyed the winters he lived in South Carolina planning and building Brookgreen Gardens. As one year went into another, the Huntingtons made their annual visits to the South Carolina coast, but they chose eventually to remain at their homes in the North rather than make the trips south.

Don Quixote by Anna Hyatt Huntington. Photo Courtesy of Brookgreen Gardens.

The Grand Strand

"I'll never be traced by the quarters I dropped."

Archer Milton Huntington died on December 11, 1955, at age 86. His father had once said of himself that he would never be traced by the quarters he dropped or the money he gave away, but the obituary of the son noted that *he* had given away much of his multimillion dollar fortune in founding and supporting museums.

Anna Hyatt Huntington spent her last years at her home in Connecticut. When she died in her ninety-eighth year in October 1973, her sculpture was being displayed all over the world.

Brookgreen Gardens Today

The trustees of Brookgreen Gardens have accepted the challenge and are dedicated to continuing the fulfillment of the purpose as stated in the Brookgreen constitution. The garden continues to grow with great acquisitions of important American sculpture set in an unparalleled wonderland of flowering plants and trees. A recent acquisition is one of the largest and most important groups of sculpture created in the twentieth century. The distinguished sculptor, Carl Milles, in 1949 had been commissioned to create a monumental fountain for The Metropolitan Museum of Art in New York City, and the theme of this fountain was the arts. He chose to call it THE FOUNTAIN OF THE MUSES, and the five artists represented are the poet, architect, musician, painter and sculptor. These male figures each carry a symbol of their chosen art, and they dash across the surface of a pool which has been formed by the fountain of the Muse, Aganippe. On either side of her are mythological creatures, a centaur and a faun. A dozen bronze pieces comprise this joyous and playful masterpiece. Working in the sculpture studio of the American Academy in Rome, Carl Milles sculpted for five years before completing THE FOUNTAIN OF THE MUSES. The size of the pool at Brookgreen is identical to that in The Metropolitan Museum. When museum directors discovered that the weight of the pool was causing a structural hazard, they began seeking an outdoors setting for the fountain. Brookgreen, with its lush gardens and terraced landscaping, was chosen as the most appropriate location for this important work of art.

Brookgreen Gardens is open daily from 9:30 AM to 4:45 PM for a moderate admission fee.

Brookgreen Gardens

Brookgreen Gardens is on the National Register of Historic Places.

Diana of the Chase by Anna Hyatt Huntington.
Photo courtesy of Brookgreen Gardens.

The Grand Strand

Photo by Heidi Hall, courtesy of *Pawleys Island Perspective*.

Huntington Beach State Park

The gate at Huntington Beach State Park, on the opposite side of U.S. 17 from the entrance to Brookgreen Gardens, opens to 2500 acres of lowcountry scenery. The road curves tunnellike through a grove of oaks icicled in gray moss. From the dimness of the surrounding old, gnarled oaks, the road leads out to an area of marshland suddenly opening up the view of water and sky. Alligators lie on the bank of the marsh and are fed chicken, pork and beef scraps about 5:00 PM each day during summer.

Atalaya

Around the next curve, near the sea, is Atalaya, the house built by Mr. and Mrs. Archer M. Huntington. This residence, as all of Huntington's, was of masonry construction. Building the dwelling of brick gave work to a great many people of the lowcountry during the days of the Great Depression. In addition, according to Huntington's friend Mosier, "Mr. Huntington believed brick to be fire-resistant. He was opposed to carrying insurance on his mansions."

The building of the house in the dunes went on for more than three years. Materials that arrived at the railroad dock in Georgetown were brought up the Waccamaw River by tugboats and off-landed at the Brookgreen landing. The house was named Atalaya, meaning castle in the sand.

Living quarters consisted of 30 rooms. There were rooms for servants, cooks, people who did the laundry, housekeepers, and secretaries. An oyster shucking room faced the ocean. A 25-foot skylight afforded natural light to Mrs. Huntington's studio in the south wing. Outside Mrs. Huntington's studio were located the stables, dog kennels and bear cages.

An inner courtyard, surrounded by the four wings of the mansion, contained 50 royal palm trees. Two identical stairways led from the courtyard to a flat roof affording a panoramic view of the sea.

Black wrought-iron grillwork, especially designed and made by Tito and Rogers of Miami, guarded the windows; and if one counted, there were 25 fireplaces. "Oh how Mr. Huntington loved an open fire," Genevieve Chandler says.

Deerhounds from Scotland

Mrs. Huntington imported deerhounds from Scotland and had an elaborate five-room house built for the dogs. "They were beautiful," Genevieve Chandler says. "There were about two dozen of them, and she would race them on the beach." Mosier remembered that the "first male and female deerhounds were brought over from Scotland, and one of them was 30 inches tall at the shoulder and weighed nearly 100 pounds. "They would put their paws on your shoulders and look you in the eye," Mosier said, "and if they didn't like you they could be quite vicious."

Maids came from Scotland

Maids and the women who did the laundry were brought to Atalaya from Scotland. "The little Scottish maids ran around, talking in their accents, and they changed linens on all the beds every morning. That was a luxury none of the rest of us could afford," Mrs. Chandler says.

Each winter, two weeks before the Huntingtons were expected for their visit to Atalaya, the maids in black uniforms and white aprons and caps "ran their legs off in the brick hallways getting everything ready for the Huntingtons." When Sundays came, the Scottish women were driven to a Presbyterian church for services.

It was not uncommon for each guest at an Atalaya dinner party to be given a beautifully wrapped gift. After the gifts were opened, cocktails that had been sweetened with honey were served. Mr. Huntington believed honey, as a natural sweetener, was not as harmful to the body as sugar. Sometime between the serving of cocktails and the finger bowls and linen towels that were brought to the guests at the end of a meal, the Huntingtons usually discussed family business matters with each other. As he sat at the head of the table and she at the other end, they talked quite loudly to each other about matters with which the guests were not acquainted.

During the last years of Huntington's life, the couple did not visit Atalaya. After the death of Mr. Huntington, most of the furniture and objects of art were moved to Mrs. Huntington's home in New York City.

Visiting Atalaya Today

Atalaya is open to the public from June 1 through Labor Day for a small fee. During spring and fall, the house is open during arts and crafts shows.

Walking along the Jetty

The South Jetty at the northern section of the beach area, along with the North Jetty at Garden City Beach, stabilizes the inlet across the ocean bar at Murrells Inlet so that commercial and recreational boats can navigate the channel at all times, regardless of the level of the tide. You can walk on the jetty and view the ocean; and from the end of the walkway, looking back, it is easy to see why the natives work so hard to keep this special place quaint and unchanged.

Huntington Beach State Park Campground

All campsites in the campground at the southern end of the park have water and electrical hookups, tables, grills and complete restroom facilities. Administered by the Division of Parks and Recreation, South Carolina Department of Parks, Recreation and Tourism, facilities include an ocean swimming area, playground equipment and carpet golf. There is a trading post (general store) and a picnic area with shelters. Daily organized nature programs include nature trail hiking and bird-watching.

For camping reservations, phone (803) 237-4440 or write Superintendent, Huntington Beach State Park, Murrells Inlet, South Carolina 29576.

"Atalaya." Photo by Sid Rhyne.

The Grand Strand

Photo by Heidi Hall, courtesy of *Pawleys Island Perspective*.

Sandy Island

The Waccamaw River portion of the Intracoastal Waterway separates Sandy Island and Brookgreen Gardens. All islands have magical qualities, but more than most, this 40-square-mile land area has its distinct personality. There are no gracious houses or spacious lawns here. Electricity came in the mid-1960s, and telephones about ten years later. There is no bridge and no ferry, and children ride a school boat back and forth to the mainland.

The People

This island lying west of the Intracoastal Waterway was covered with great plantations in the 1800s. They were Oak Hampton, Ruinville, Mount Arena, Sandy Knowe, Oak Lawn, Holly Hill, Pipe Down, Grove Hill and Hasell Hill. Some evidence of the former plantations survives. Many of the 250 Sandy Islanders are descendants of slaves who worked in plantation rice fields, and some of the descendants speak Gullah, a Creole patois spoken in Sandy Island rice fields. Their customs and beliefs cannot be trifled with. The people on Sandy Island today are hard-working, middle-class people.

Plans for Development

In the early 1970s, a real estate development company made plans to build houses on Sandy Island, but due to difficulties with permits and zoning laws the plans were dropped. About the same time, the county embarked on a ferry project. The islanders were overjoyed at the prospect of having a ferry. Crossing the rivers is one of their major problems. "When it rains we get wet," one resident says. "If the wind's a-blowin', it'll blow you out of the boat." And there was a plan for a bridge that would connect the island to Bucksport. But the costly projects were abandoned.

Visitors can see Sandy Island from boats that offer Waccamaw River tours. The boats leave from the Wacca Wache Marina at Murrells Inlet and the bridge in Socastee.

The Grand Strand

Sandy Island school boat.
Photo by Heidi Hall, courtesy of *Pawleys Island Perspective*.

Litchfield Beach

Today Litchfield Beach is a well-polished resort that may outdazzle some others, but it was once a remote part of the peninsula between the Waccamaw River and the ocean.

Slaves and their descendants who lived on this part of the coast used ingredients gathered in woods and marshes to make medicine. A bitter tea was made from weeds that caused profuse perspiration and usually proved effective for certain maladies, including fever. An iron tonic said to invigorate the physically weak was made by gathering cinders from a blacksmith's shop, pounding them into fine powder and mixing them with molasses and ginger to make the concoction palatable. Syrup, ginger and soda made a cough remedy. Cherokee root, oak bark and whiskey, when mixed together, made a general tonic.

Resort Attractions

Development of this beach began after World War II, and today the beach is famous for the inn and country club, which offer tennis, golf and live entertainment in an oceanfront lounge. Rooms in the inn are among the most up-to-the-minute in decor and facilities on the Grand Strand. And the dining room is a wonderful place to enjoy cuisine from the sea and from the land.

Villas have sprung up almost like marsh grass. A residential area named Litchfield by the Sea is blessed not only with a salt marsh, but with nearly one mile of ocean beach.

Splendid Plantation

Litchfield Plantation, a private residential community on S.C. 255 about three miles inland, looks much as it did during the days when the Tuckers planted rice there. Peter Simons left Litchfield to his son, John, who sold it to Daniel Tucker around 1795. The Tucker family came to South Carolina from Bermuda, and the title to the property remained in the Tucker name until 1904. The mansion built in 1794 still stands in splendor. A house

The Grand Strand

on the ocean at Litchfield Beach is maintained for use by the owners of condominiums and houses located on Litchfield Plantation property. Litchfield Plantation is not open to the public.

Litchfield Plantation photo by Sid Rhyne.

Pawleys Island

Pawleys Island is a mere speck of land off the coast of South Carolina near U.S. 17, 25 miles south of Myrtle Beach. It was named for George, Anthony and Percival Pawley, sons of Percival Pawley I, who took a grant to land here in 1711. At its widest point, the island is no more than one-fourth mile across, and it is less than four miles long. Eighteenth-century beach houses of some of the rice planters have managed to survive neglect and hurricanes, builders and bulldozers. Therein lies the heritage and charm of Pawleys Island, which is on the National Register of Historic Places.

Relief from "Summer Fever"

Planter families came here during the summer months for the therapeutic effects of salt water and sea air. The humid, stagnant air in the rice fields infected the people with "summer fever" (malaria) if they remained there. August and September, when the swamps were filled with mosquitoes, were called "the sickly months." Among prominent families who found summer relief at Pawleys Island were the Allstons, Labruces, Tuckers, Westons and Wards.

Cypress timber for construction of the houses was hewn on the plantations and taken to the island by boat. Roman numerals were chiseled on beams and boards so that they could be easily matched when they arrived at the site of construction. The houses had wraparound porches and kitchens separate from the house. (The old whitewashed houses are easily recognized today.)

Planter families were rowed to Pawleys Island by oarsmen who sang as they pulled on the oars. From their rowing songs other music inevitably came. The beginnings of simple melodies, intricate rhythms and forceful harmonies doubtless came from Africa, and there was no more beautiful music in the world than that music developed by slaves as they rowed their masters to Pawleys Island. Among the spirituals the oarsmen sang on the Pee Dee and Waccamaw rivers were "Roll, Jordan, Roll" and "O Zion."

The Grand Strand

Children of the planters were required to read and write during their vacations. They read the classics in the mornings and were not allowed to read works of their own choosing until 3:00 PM They made daily records in journals of their vacations at Pawleys. Many servants accompanied planter families to the island. There were cooks, butlers, seamstresses and nurses for the children. There was much visiting back and forth between vacationing families, and this custom carried over into the next century. In the early 1900s, an orchestra came from Georgetown to play for dancing and parties held during summer vacations.

By 1920 carriages had been replaced by automobiles in Pawleys Island driveways, and by 1940 Pawleys Island was known as the place to be invited to a college house party—especially during Easter vacation. A pavilion was constructed over a section of the marsh.

Excellent Fishing

The Pawleys pier, built in 1952, provided excellent fishing and also served to divide the island into two sections: North Pawleys and South Pawleys. However, the pier is no longer open to the public because it is a part of Pawleys Pier Village, a condominium complex. South of the pier, jetties jut into the breakers and prevent beach erosion, and to the north sand slopes to the surf.

Creek at Pawleys Island.
Photo by Joseph Hayes, courtesy of *Pawleys Island Perspective*.

Pawleys Island

Change has been slow at Pawleys. Old-timers recline in the hammocks that hang on the porches and talk about the time they sampled apple wine at Davis' Store, or sneaked into The Towers (better known as The Temple of Dionysus of the Island) or danced at the old pavilion, which burned, and later at the new pavilion, which also burned. But newcomers are showing up on the island each year, and cottages, apartments and condominiums are rented through local rental agencies.

All Saints Church

During the years of rice planting, the church was the axis in the lives of the people on plantations. In this parish they attended All Saints Waccamaw Episcopal Church on S.C. 255, about three miles west of Pawleys Island. Exterior design of the present church is much like that of the church on this site that burned to the ground on December 12, 1915. The interior differs. Straight pews were installed rather than box pews and, of course, there is no slave gallery as before. Carvings in the cemetery by the church hint at past drama in old lives. Shaded from the sun, the stones reveal that the hurricane of October 13, 1893, took the lives of some members of this church. Under an oak tree is a monument in memory of George Pawley, who donated the land for this church. Plowden Weston's burying place is a few steps away. Words chiseled in stone say he fell asleep in January 25, 1864, at age forty-four. Grave markers for the Wards of Brookgreen are at the back of the cemetery.

Photo by La'tka Thompson, courtesy of *Pawleys Island Perspective*.

The Grand Strand

The Hammock Shop

Back on U.S. 17, shopping is at its best. Need a cross-stitch sampler, delicate linen, Pawleys Island corn relish, hot pepper jelly or designer lingerie? How about an old map, out-of-print book, original watercolor of the ancient houses on the island or an original Pawleys Island hammock? Try the Hammock Shop on U.S. 17 at the causeway. Exclusive shops sell almost everything you would want and everything Grandma would want, including made-on-the-premises rope hammocks. Nearly 2000 people on a summer day shop at the original manufacturing site of the world-famous rope hammocks.

When Joshua Ward of Brookgreen found the going rough as he transported rice to market by boat, he designed a rope hammock. The hanging lounge was so cool and comfortable that Ward's brother-in-law, A. H. Lachicotte (LASH-ey-cot) and his wife made some and sold them by the roadside. This successful venture was the start of today's Hammock Shop.

At the end of World War II, A. H. "Doc" Lachicotte, Jr., a son, returned home and added another building as well as a nursery where he sold lowcountry shrubbery. The nursery was later phased out to make room for additional shops. Although hammocks are the most popular item (the retail coordinator for them estimates 50,000 are sold yearly), all of the shops in the complex are uncommonly successful. Part of the success formula is "Doc" Lachicotte's imposed condition that all stores have a lowcountry, rice planter, plantation design—high-pitched, shingled or tin roofs, construction from lumber taken from plantation mansions or rice mills, whitewashed wood. An authentic tobacco barn and a plantation schoolhouse are part of the compound. The Pawleys Island Inn is a two-story building in the design of a plantation manor house. Candles in the restaurant throw flickering light on ancient brick and wood. Language on the menu is endearingly Pawleys Island: soups include He Crab; the favorite sandwich is Little "Doc" Special; and desserts are called All Saints Indulgences. Desserts include Susan's Derby Pie and Libba's Lemon Butter Tart.

One hundred years after Joshua Ward designed his hammock, tourists have Pawleys Island Hammock Shop fever. The greatest expansion of all has been in the parking area.

The Island Shops

Across U.S. 17 from the Hammock Shop is another shopping complex—The Island Shops. Here one can buy colorful Lilly

Pawleys Island

Pulitzer sportswear like that seen on Grand Strand golf courses. The Mole Hole is a gift shop in the group of gray buildings.

Accommodations at Pawleys Island are sparse. Ancient records tell us that "the quality" came to this beach before the Revolutionary War, and today's residents put forth stringent efforts to avoid all publicity. Bedrooms for rent at Pawleys Island are usually reserved far in advance of the summer season. One of the old houses that was made into a guest house is the Pelican Inn, long ago the summer home of Plowden C. J. Weston of Hagley Plantation.

The Grand Strand

Arcadia Plantation House photo by Sid Rhyne.

Debordieu Colony Club

Many global trend-setters have houses at Debordieu Colony Club, a private residential area by the seashore on the east of U.S. 17 between Pawleys Island and Georgetown. Unless you have friends who live at Debordieu, there is a slim chance you will be granted entry. Word from the gate house to sightseers is usually "Sorry, but you cannot go in."

Mrs. Wallace Pate inherited this property, as well as Arcadia Plantation on the western side of U.S. 17, from her late father, George Vanderbilt. The Pates live at Arcadia Plantation house, a house that makes some of the mansions in *Gone With The Wind* pallid by comparison.

A golf course takes up some of the 2600 acres of Debordieu, and there are also a few condominiums.

An archaeological dig was conducted on this acreage by a professor from Coastal Carolina College. Hundreds of ancient artifacts were uncovered in the dig.

The Grand Strand

Hobcaw Barony House photo by Heidi Hall, courtesy of *Pawleys Island Perspective*.

Hobcaw Barony

Hobcaw Barony is a spread of about 17,000 acres, some of which jut into Winyah Bay at Georgetown. There are 80 miles of roadways on the plantation beyond the entrance gates by U.S. 17. It is more than a typical plantation, even for a country squire whose lineage was long and strong and who amassed a fortune on Wall Street. Two beautifully landscaped and furnished houses are on the property. A general tour, at $3.00 per person, is offered on Thursday mornings, from 9 to 12, by reservation only. Guests are transported by van and see such historic sites as Hobcaw House, Friendfield Village (old slave street), Marine Laboratory, Cypress Swamp and Clambank Landing.

After becoming a millionaire, in 1905 Bernard Baruch began piecing together the original Hobcaw Barony that had been one of Carolina's largest land tracts granted to John, Lord Carteret, one of the Lords Proprietors. Acquiring plantations that had belonged to Hugers, Alstons, Heriots, and other South Carolina landed gentry, Baruch purchased even more land than had been a part of the original king's grant.

Churchill and Roosevelt

Baruch and his family wintered in a large Victorian mansion at Hobcaw named Friendfield House. The Baruch children loved Friendfield for its hominess, something they said their New York home lacked. As the family entertained guests at Christmas dinner in 1929, the house was engulfed in flames, and the people escaped to the lawn where they watched as the structure burned to the ground. Baruch built a new residence overlooking Winyah Bay. Hobcaw House was constructed of brick, steel and concrete to make it as fireproof as possible. It was in this house that Baruch entertained Sir Winston Churchill and his daughter Diana and President Franklin D. Roosevelt. Many other famous people were guests at Hobcaw House.

Roosevelt's health was failing when he made his last visit to

The Grand Strand

Hobcaw in the spring of 1944. This was a time of great peril as World War II was flaming in Europe. Roosevelt traveled in strictest secrecy, and soldiers in camouflaged uniforms were stationed in the forests for reasons of security. The president seemed to enjoy talking with descendants of former slaves, listening to their singing in a small church and watching them dance in a barn. Those who saw Roosevelt at that time said he seemed to relax and gain strength. Each afternoon he visited Baruch's daughter Belle at Bellefield, her plantation home on Hobcaw property. The room in which Belle and Roosevelt talked away the afternoons has a lofty ceiling with exposed wood beams to which stuffed animals and deer antlers are attached. Photographs of famous people adorn a grand piano in the living room. A photograph of President Roosevelt is inscribed, "To Belle, for the charming house, with regards, Franklin D. Roosevelt."

Bernard Baruch gave title to Hobcaw Barony to Belle in 1958, and she began to make plans for the property. She desired that after the deaths of her father and herself the property be used for the purpose of teaching and/or research in forestry, marine biology, and the care and propagation of wildlife and flora and fauna. Six years later Belle Baruch died and her father died a year later.

Under the terms of Belle Baruch's will, Clemson University assumed responsibility for conducting research and teaching forestry and wildlife management science, and the University of South Carolina became responsible for research and teaching in marine and coastal areas.

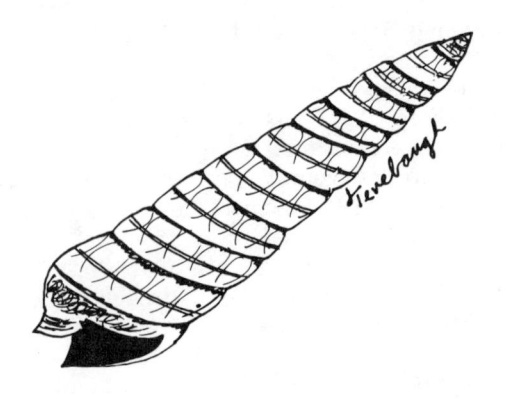

Georgetown

Georgetown, 35 miles south of Myrtle Beach on U.S. 17, is the southernmost point of the Grand Strand. This town is located on Winyah Bay where the Waccamaw, Black, Pee Dee and Sampit rivers meet. The area is rich in history and tradition; the city of Georgetown Historic District is on the National Register of Historic Places.

The Church of Prince George Winyah

The most historic building in Georgetown is the Church of Prince George Winyah at the corner of Broad and Highmarket streets. The building, named for the Prince of Wales who became George II, has been in use since the middle of the 1700s. The British occupied the building during the Revolutionary War; they first used it as a stable, then burned it. After that war a new roof was added and new pews were installed. A marble baptismal font was taken from the church during the Civil War. The font was later found in a cabin where it had been used for the pounding of rice. It was restored and returned to the church in 1866. The stained glass window in back of the altar was once in St. Mary's Chapel at Hagley Plantation near Pawleys Island. Plowden C. J. Weston of Hagley Plantation gave the window and the bell in the tower to Prince George Winyah. The church and adjoining cemetery are on the National Register of Historic Places.

The Old Slave Market

The Rice Museum is located in a building that is also on the National Register of Historic Places—the Old Slave Market on Front Street. This structure was erected on the exact site of a similar building that had been destroyed by a hurricane in 1822. The Old Slave Market with a clock in the steeple was patterned after the Town Hall and Clock Building in Keswick, England. It has been used as a jail, printing shop and police department, as well as a slave market. The city of Georgetown has made the building available to be used as a museum. In the museum, the

The Grand Strand

visitor follows the cultivation of rice from the construction of the fields with their ditches, dikes and trunk docks to the shipping of the product to ports throughout the world. The cultivation of rice required an almost unending supply of labor, from the humblest task of weeding the fields and shooing away birds to the skilled labor of the plantation artisans.

Winyah Indigo Society Hall

The architecturally interesting Winyah Indigo Society Hall on the corner of Prince and Cannon streets is not open to the public; it is still in use as a meeting place for members of the society. This society was incorporated by an act of Parliament on May 21, 1757, for the purpose of educating the children of the region. Thomas Lynch, Sr., father of the signer of the Declaration of Independence, was the first president. But the society began as a convivial club formed about 1740 by Georgetown District planters of indigo. The gatherings were lively; members discussed the latest news from England as well as the production of indigo.

Indigo as a product had been perfected in the West Indies; from there it came to the coast of South Carolina. The indigo plant produces a blue dye, and it has been said that no chemically-produced dye has replaced the soft shades of blue from the indigo plant.

Slaves were allowed to have for themselves the skim that rose to the top of the vats. The "skimmins" were a prize for it was believed by the people born in slavery that if they painted the frames of their doors and windows with the blue dye, evil spirits would not enter. Some cabins in the lowcountry still have door and window frames painted blue. The market for indigo suffered after the American Revolution due to cheaper markets developing in other parts of the world, but the vast wealth that had been amassed from the production of this product was the foundation of some fortunes that remain in the South Carolina lowcountry.

The Winyah Academy began in the building that stands today. The school was especially noted for its scholarly teachers of Latin and Greek. The academy was in the doldrums for a time after the Civil War; but it was restored to its former reputation, and its alumni went on to become associated with important firms around the country. Although the Winyah Indigo Society is still in existence and has meetings several times a year, it has been many years since a school has been operated by the society.

Georgetown

The Winyah Indigo Society Hall was designed by Edward Brickell White, who also designed the Huguenot Church in Charleston and Trinity Episcopal Church in Columbia.

According to the legal surveyor's map of Georgetown, most Georgetown houses are on lots measuring 100 X 217.9, as laid out by William Swinton, a surveyor who divided the acreage into blocks containing a total of 230 lots in 1734. Townhouses of the planters are evident on the streets of the historic district. The streets are Screven, Highmarket, Queen, Broad, King, Prince, Orange, Cannon, St. James and Front. A map of these streets and the houses on them can be obtained from the chamber of commerce offices on Front Street.

Photo by Sid Rhyne.

The Grand Strand

The Kaminski House

The Harold Kaminski House on Front Street can be toured. It was built around 1760 and overlooks the Sampit River. The house sits perpendicular to the street, and its wide piazza, which extends the length of the building, is barely visible from the street.

In the house are so many heirloom pieces that one would have difficulty singling out individual antiques to describe. A family of Kaminskis were prominent in Georgetown in the 1800s, and Mrs. Kaminski's family, the Pyatts, an English family, had been among the first settlers. Most visitors entering the front hall show special interest in a fifteenth-century Spanish chest made of oak and walnut. The chest at one time belonged to Don Pedro of Brazil. Also in the front hall are a pair of Acajou French Empire side chairs, a grandfather clock and a rare Beluchistan rug.

The dining room was the scene of many dinners served ceremoniously as guests sat at the mahogany Chippendale design banquet table that runs almost the entire length of the room. The sixteen matched Duncan Phyfe chairs with carved leaves are in place, and exceptionally beautiful china with the Pyatt coat of arms is on the table as though guests are expected at any minute. An American Empire sideboard, an antique mahogany Chippendale corner cabinet with original brass pulls, and an American Empire china cupboard hold additional china. Dr. Chalmers G. Davidson, archivist of the E. H. Little Library at Davidson College, remembers having dinner there:

> "Dinner at Julia Kaminski's was a never-to-be-forgotten experience. I'm not sure everybody got the five-course treatment (after all, I was writing a book including her fabulous Pyatt forebears!) [*The Last Foray*, University of South Carolina Press, 1971], but I've heard of others equally speechless. We began with the soup course, and that was removed for the salad. Then came the fish course, as only Georgetonians can serve it (I was never quite sure what it was). After that, the meat and vegetables, local products, locally flourished. And finally a dessert which floated on your palate, here again I was not sure of the ingredients. The

cloth was removed for fruit, nuts and finger bowls. Then we could smoke. No one would have had the bad taste to do it before or during a Kaminski dinner."

Mr. and Mrs. Harold Kaminski are deceased. Their home is open to the public Tuesday through Friday, 10:00 AM to 4:00 PM.

International Paper Company

In the 1800s, the Atlantic coast Lumber Company opened the largest sawmill in the world at Georgetown, producing over one-half million feet of lumber per day. To say that this mill gave the place a boost in economy is a distinct understatement. A majority of the Georgetown County residents depended on the sawmill for their living. But the Atlantic Coast Lumber Company shut down permanently when the Depression reached the area in 1932. It is ironic that during that very time the International Paper Corp. was expanding its operations in the South. An article in The Georgetown Times in 1936 reported a massive $8 million paper mill was under construction.

During the first month of paper mill operation, the population of Georgetown increased by more than 3000. In 1937 when the mill began papermaking operations, there were 1215 people working in the mill. Five hundred ninety-three cords of wood were consumed daily in the production of 263 tons of paper.

Today the International Paper Corp. is a massive forest prod-

Photo by Sid Rhyne.

The Grand Strand

ucts business with operations in 38 states, including 15 pulp and paper mills and more than 31,000 employees.

Georgetown Steel Corporation

During the warm days of July 1969, the first heat of steel was melted in one of Georgetown Steel Corporation's two electric arc furnaces, starting a new industry that would be vital to the economy of this town.

The mill has an annual capacity of approximately 600,000 tons and produces small-diameter, close-tolerance wire rods, coiled small-diameter reinforcing bar and special quality bars. The 40-acre plant site is on the Sampit River in downtown Georgetown.

Georgetown Harbor

As early as 1723, the people of this place petitioned for a port of entry. The Assembly urged its committee of correspondence to write the South Carolina agent in London to secure such a designation for Winyah. If Winyah were made a port of entry, they said, local produce could be shipped directly to a foreign destination and the shippers would be free of burdensome freight charges to Charleston. "Tho we have paid so many taxes, yet none of it is applied to our services in order to make a port," the people wrote.

Robert Johnson, when he became royal governor, was determined to solve this problem. On January 1, 1730, he wrote a memorandum to the British Government: "First as there are many people now settled upon the River of Winyiah, I conceive it to be necessary to lay out a town, make it a port of entry and appoint a collector there."

In 1731 the royal authorities acted to make Georgetown a port of entry; Peter Goudett was appointed naval officer and collector. The naval officer was responsible for keeping a register of the vessels that arrived and departed at this port, quarterly sending a copy of the register to Charleston.

The first full year of seaport trade, from November 1, 1733, to November, 1734, was typical of the early years. Three sloops cleared for Charleston; five sloops, a schooner and a brigantine for Philadelphia; three sloops for Boston; and one for Bermuda. Three snows and one brigantine sailed for Poole, three ships directly for London, and one for Bristol. Rice and fruit were taken to Charleston, while pitch, tar and turpentine were shipped to other ports.

Georgetown

There has been a steady increase in the use of Georgetown's port facilities since the days of rice culture. More than 2000 pleasure boats are serviced each year at the Georgetown dock, and charter boats leave this harbor to take fishing parties to off-shore fishing sites.

Georgetown Tour Train

To review three centuries of history of Georgetown, tourists board the Tour Train at the chamber of commerce office, 600 Front Street. (The train is more of a carriage that is pulled by another vehicle.) For a fee, one can ride at a leisurely pace through 220 acres of this historic city. The train stops at Prince George Winyah Episcopal Church, where a tour of the church and cemetery are given by a local guide.

Plantation Tours

Each spring, usually in April, the women of Prince George Winyah Episcopal Church sponsor tours of plantations on the Pee Dee, Black, Sampit, Waccamaw and Santee rivers. Some town houses in Georgetown are open for the tours, as well as the Winyah Indigo Society Hall and several churches. The plantations are open from 10:00 AM to 6:00 PM; box lunches and tickets for the tours can be purchased at the church at Broad and Highmarket streets. For more information on the plantation tours, write Women of the Church, Prince George Winyah Episcopal Church, Georgetown, South Carolina 29440. Or phone the chamber of commerce at (803) 546-8436.

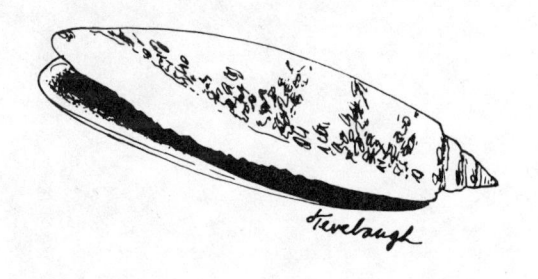

The Grand Strand

Georgetown Harbor photo by Sid Rhyne.

Yawkey Wildlife Center

Off the coast of southeastern Georgetown, right about where Winyah Bay bumps into the Atlantic Ocean, there are three islands named North, South and Cat. Around them marshland rolls up into forests of hardwoods. For more than 50 years, the islands comprising about 20,000 acres belonged to Tom Yawkey, who also owned the Boston Red Sox Baseball Club. Under the will of Tom Yawkey, the property went to the South Carolina Wildlife and Marine Resources Department in 1976. Along with the property, a $10 million trust fund was left to the trustees of Tom Yawkey Wildlife Center. The property and trust fund is considered one of the most outstanding gifts to wildlife conservation in North America.

During the years Yawkey managed his islands, the land earned the reputation as one of the most outstanding wildlife refuges on the Atlantic. Where Tom Yawkey roamed, eagles still soar, ospreys occupy the same nests, and heaven seems to peek at the open marshland where old-time rice trunk docks prevent inlet water from overflowing into former rice fields.

Tom Yawkey was a special man. When his house burned, he had two small mobile homes moved to South Island and placed so that they faced each other. Yawkey and his wife lived in the trailers while the superintendent of Yawkey's islands lived in a graceful, two-story white house in a grove of trees. Yawkey was asked why he didn't have the superintendent move so that he and Mrs. Yawkey could live in the stately house. "Why I can't do that!" Yawkey exclaimed. "That's the superintendent's house!" For the rest of his days, when they were at their island retreat, the Yawkeys resided in the trailers; to this day the superintendent lives in the white house.

The superintendent, or project leader/resident biologist, is Robert L. Joyner. In running the refuge, he keeps a twentieth-century pace with an impressive mixture of machinery, business acumen and level-eyed pride. When Joyner first met Yawkey, Joyner didn't know with whom he was talking. Yawkey questioned the young man at length on the flora and fauna of

The Grand Strand

the estuaries and on wildlife management. Joyner fired back the answers, his alert eyes twinkling. It wasn't long before he was managing the place. Joyner personally conducts one tour of the refuge each week.

Joyner's Tours

Yawkey's name comes up frequently in Joyner's lecture as he drives over the property. He explains that Yawkey inherited the property in 1919 from an uncle who owned the Detroit Tigers Baseball Club. The nephew took much the same path as the uncle – not only in revering the islands, but he went on to buy the Boston Red Sox.

Yawkey's Will

In his will, Tom Yawkey specified that his property be used for wildlife management, conservation and education. It was especially dedicated as a habitat for wintering waterfowl, although five endangered species of wildlife live on the islands: red cockaded woodpecker, alligator, brown pelican, loggerhead turtle and bald eagle.

Obtaining Permission for a Tour

Tom Yawkey Wildlife Center is operated on the same predication that Yawkey asserted: That too many people and wildlife do not mix, and on his property, wildlife would come first. Therefore, visits to the property offshore from the end of South Island Road, which leaves U.S. 17 south of the Sampit River bridge, should be restricted to at least one of the four purposes to which the Center is dedicated:

- Approved research
- Nature study
- Educational field trips
- Conservation management study

To inquire about a visit, write to Robert L. Joyner, Tom Yawkey Wildlife Center, Route 2, Georgetown, South Carolina 29440.

Group size is limited to 14 persons, and no more than one tour a week is usually scheduled.

Socastee

West of the Grand Strand resort area on S.C. 544 is a village that is far enough away from the bustling activity to live according to old rhythms of season and water.

Socastee takes its name from a tribe of Indians. The swamp that also took this name extends along the Intracoastal Waterway for several miles. The Socastee portion of the Intracoastal Waterway is known as the Pine Island Cut and was the last section of the waterway to be built.

A Quiet Place

Peace. Quiet. A feeling of timelessness. A sense of suspension in some Old World moment. That's what you get on a stroll through Socastee. Here was where Jeremiah Smith produced a fine crop of Jersey Wakefield cabbage, and where barrels of turpentine were hauled by wagon three miles to Peach Tree Landing where they were loaded on flat boats and floated down the river. One can breathe the romance of a time that was, but times are changing. More and more, people are opting to live near Socastee rather than closer to the beaches. Prices of real estate are going up.

Oregon Plantation

One of the lowcountry's most tragic tales is the story of a cruel overseer at Oregon Plantation located at Enterprise. Ben Horry's father was Joshua John Ward's driver at Brookgreen. Ben told this story:

> "They said people been running away from Oregon Plantation at Enterprise. That mean overseer! They say that after freedom came they [former slaves] put four horses to him. One to every limb. Stretch him! Then they cut the horses loose, and each horse carried a piece of the overseer."

Oregon Plantation was one of the few plantations in Horry

The Grand Strand

County. It consisted of 248 acres of rice land and 4000 acres of pine land. Symbolic of the collapse of the rice economy between 1893 and 1911 was the decline of many of the Waccamaw River plantations. Oregon Plantation is no longer in existence as a plantation.

Once a Thriving Village

Socastee is a small village, not thriving as it once was. The first church here was a log building with wooden shutters. Metal holders on the walls contained the candles that lit the church. Women of the church made candles of beeswax.

The first school in Horry County was located at Socastee. Some of Horry's most prominent citizens received their education at the Socastee Academy, built on the south side of Socastee Creek on the site of the present Socastee High School.

Until U.S. 501 was built in 1948, the Conway-Socastee-Myrtle Beach road was the major route into Myrtle Beach. People came to this place on Saturdays to buy supplies, including nails, medicines, cloth, buttons and trimmings, as well as fertilizer and farming tools.

General Merchandise Store

The old gray general merchandise store of T. B. Cooper is no longer open, but the building still stands near the drawbridge. On the porch one can breathe the romance of times that were. This old-time store provided everyday necessities, as well as a place to meet friends and pass and receive news of neighbors. At one time, a post office was in back. It was separated from the merchandise by a heavy wire grille. A safe behind the grille was used for the safekeeping of valuables, documents and cash collected in the store. Rumor has it that the grille and the safe are still there in the store that sits in repose. Be sure to note the double doors and shuttered windows of the 80-foot long building.

Conway

Conway, 14 miles west of Myrtle Beach on U.S. 501, is the third name of the county seat of Horry County. When the town was laid out by Alexander Skene and Chief Justice Wright in 1734, it was named Kingston. The name was changed to Conwayborough in 1802 in honor of Robert Conway, a colonel who fought in the Revolution with Francis Marion; and in 1884 an act was passed to drop the *borough*.

The Gun Was Loaded

Mail arrived by messengers on foot or horseback and by boat, and it was not until a railroad was built that mail was delivered here daily. The first railroad built here was the Wilmington, Chadbourn & Conway Line. In 1887 this railroad company obtained permission from the Horry County Board of Commissioners to lay its track along Main Street for a distance of about 1500 feet. During construction of this length of track, Mary Beaty walked from her house on Main Street, raised a gun, and ordered the crew to move the right-of-way in order to preserve two live oak trees. The men laying the track concurred. The gun was loaded.

The Atlantic Coast Line bought out the existing railroad in 1912. By that time the railroad on Main Street had become a nuisance. The town council passed an ordinance limiting the actions of the trains in the downtown area, and the section of track running through the business district of Main Street was removed.

Buildings in this town were updated after World War I when veterans returned with some new ideas. The state highway system was established in 1924, and this further encouraged development.

City Hall Built in 1824

When you see the city hall on the corner of Main Street and Third Avenue, take the time to stop and thoroughly look it over. Built in 1824, the building was designed by Robert Mills, the

The Grand Strand

designer of the Washington Monument and other public buildings in the nation's capital. The public building is brick with vaulted record rooms. Rod ties on the exterior of the building were laced through to hold the structure together in the event of an earthquake. This building was first used as a courthouse. In 1907 it was sold to Conway for a town hall and the present courthouse was erected. The Conway City Hall is on the National Register of Historic Places.

Also see the courthouse on Third Avenue. The brick building was extensively renovated in 1966. Visitors to Conway usually seek out the Horry County Memorial Library and First Methodist Church on Fifth Avenue, considered to be among Conway's most beautiful buildings.

Conway has some attention-grabbing street names. Racepath Avenue which crosses U.S. 501 in the downtown area, got its name because horse races were held here many years ago. Just beyond Racepath at Ninth Avenue is Gasoline Alley. In 1890, when the population of Conway was less than 800, Sawdust Road made up a part of the winding road that ran between Gully Store and the shipyard; Sawdust Road is now Lakeside Drive. "The Gully" was a portion of Conway that bordered Deep Gully Branch. There were blacksmith and wheelwright shops and turpentine stills on "The Gully."

Other Conway landmarks include the historic Kingston Presbyterian Church on Third Avenue, and the road that was built around a live oak tree at 6th Ave. and Elm Street.

Colleges Near Conway

Higher education in Horry County began on July 23, 1954, when the Coastal Education Foundation was formed. Five years later, The Horry county Higher Education Commission, a spin-off of CEF, was created by statute. The two groups organized Coastal Carolina Junior College, an educational institution that entered into a contract with the University of South Carolina and later became a four-year branch of the university with authority to award Baccalaureate degrees in several areas. Today more than 2600 full-time and part-time students are enrolled in the coeducational, liberal arts curriculum. The 185-acre campus is between U.S. 501 and U.S. 544, four miles east of Conway and nine miles west of Myrtle Beach.

Horry-Georgetown Technical College

Horry-Georgetown Technical College (TEC) began operation

Conway

in September 1966 as Horry-Marion-Georgetown Technical Education Center. In 1969 the name was changed to Horry-Georgetown Technical College. The statement of purpose sets out in part that the college provide technical, industrial, business and continuing education training programs for interested and qualified students, both young and adult.

The technical college is located on U.S. 501, four miles east of Conway and nine miles west of Myrtle Beach, near Coastal Carolina College. It is fully accredited by the Southern Association of Colleges and Schools. A satellite campus is located in Georgetown on U.S. 17 south.

Horry County Museum

See the stuffed, 490-lb. black bear struck dead by an auto on U.S. 501 in 1981. Other exhibits include antique woodworking, old-time methods of logging, and the making of turpentine and tar. Located at Fifth and Main streets in Conway. Open 1-5 Mon. through Fri. and 10 to 5 on Saturday. Nominal fee.

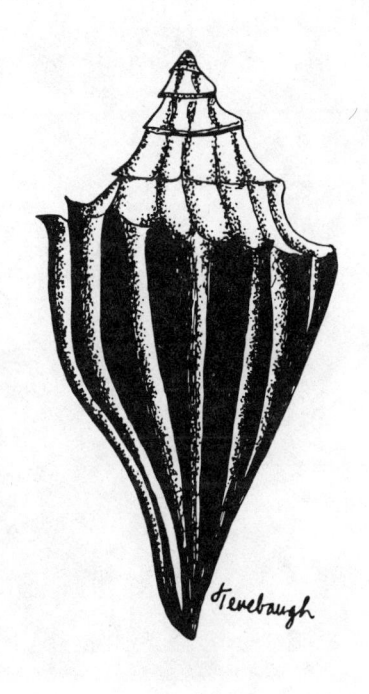

The Grand Strand

Hebron Methodist Church photo by Sid Rhyne.

Bucksport

Henry Buck found his way to Horry County from Bucksport, Maine, and perceived the potential of marketing the virgin pine, white oak and cypress lumber so abundant by the Waccamaw River. He established three sawmills on the Waccamaw, naming them Upper Mill, Middle Mill and Lower Mill. Upper Mill was later named Buck's Mill; Middle Mill became Bucksville; and Lower Mill is Bucksport, approximately ten miles south of Conway off U.S. 701 on County Road 48.

Buck had oaks and pines squared, pulled to the river and floated down to his mills for finishing and shipping. Some of the trunks of the trees taken from the forests to the mills weighed several tons. Much of the lumber went to New England where it was used in the construction of sailing vessels.

Buck brought shipwrights from Maine and offered them the services of his slaves. The workers built boats, a two-story barn, about twenty cabins for employees, an ice house, and the Hebron Methodist Church.

The Henrietta

In September 1874, Captain Jonathan Nichols and master-builder Elishua Dunbar came from Maine with 115 carpenters, blacksmiths, joiners and riggers to build *The Henrietta*, the largest ship ever to be built at Bucksville. As a test to determine whether such ships could be built more economically in Maine or on the Waccamaw, a vessel of the same model and dimensions as *The Henrietta* was constructed in Maine at the time the ship was being built at Bucksville. The cost of building the Bucksville vessel was $90,000. It required 1,300,300 feet of lumber. Cost of the sister ship built in Maine was $115,000.

Captain Andrew M. Ross was in command of *The Henrietta* in November 1890 when she sailed from New York for Portland, Oregon. His wife and three daughters were also on board. During the time the ship was in Portland, she was toured by President Harrison. The ship's captain's wife and daughters remained on board when she sailed to Melbourne, Australia, and from there to Boston where Mrs. Ross and her daughters left the ship. From Boston, *The Henrietta* took a load of lumber to Buenos Aires and then sailed back to New York where she was loaded with oil bound for Singapore. Back in New York, the vessel had a load of general cargo when she set sail for Yokahama. In August, 1894, *The Henrietta* was loaded with 800 tons of manganese ore, that tricky cargo that often shifts its weight causing imbalance of a craft.

Entering the harbor at Kobe from Yokahama where she would be loaded with more cargo before sailing for New York, *The Henrietta* encountered a violent typhoon. The pilot ran her back to an area of the sea considered secure for anchorage. Turbulent winds tore wildly at the masts, and before the storm subsided, the vessel was a total loss. All hands were saved.

The Henrietta is on the National Register of Historic Places *in absentia*.

Road's End

At Bucksport, see Road's End, a house built by Henry Buck that is now unoccupied and neglected. Buck's son, Henry Lee, and his wife, Georgia, who were married in 1866, lived in this house, and their six children were all born here.

Plantation Square and a Restaurant

Red-shingled, tin-roofed Plantation Square is a country store that invites browsing. And a restaurant on the Waccamaw River offers seafood in the evenings from 5:00 PM to 10:00 PM. The restaurant opens at 11:00 AM on Sunday.

Hebron Methodist Church

The Hebron Methodist Church is located two and a half miles off U.S. 701 on S.C. 475, 8 miles south of Conway. The simple Greek Revival church was built in 1848 of heart cypress and pine, with interior walls of oyster plaster. The original floorboards extend the entire width of the building. Windows, doors and shutters, gifts of a sea captain, came from New England. The pulpit is of Honduras mahogany and is located between the two front doors. As in other churches of that era, a partition divides the pews. Men sat on one side and women on the other.

The red-painted church is on the National Register of Historic Places. Services are held here in the building that has survived turbulent wars, economic ruptures and the ravages of coastal storms. An ancient organ is still in use.

Buck Family Cemetery

No visit to Hebron Church would be complete without a stroll through the Buck Family Cemetery across the road. Remains of this family lie in the burying ground enclosed by a fence of old brick and wrought iron.

Inscribed on a tablet in the back wall of the fence are these words:

> "Here in the Buck Family Cemetery lies Henry Buck, 1800-1870, descendant of Jonathan Buck, 1719-1775, founder of Bucksport, Maine, in the year 1762. Also here lie other pioneers and their descendants securely enshrouded in the historic soil of South Carolina."

This is Lucinda Buck's resting-place inscription:

> "Life stole away without warning;
> Said not good night!
> But in a brighter clime bade her
> Good Morning!
> She sleeps beneath her native earth,
> and near the spot where she gave birth,
> Her youthful feet trod flowers that bloom
> in beauty o'er early tomb."

The Grand Strand

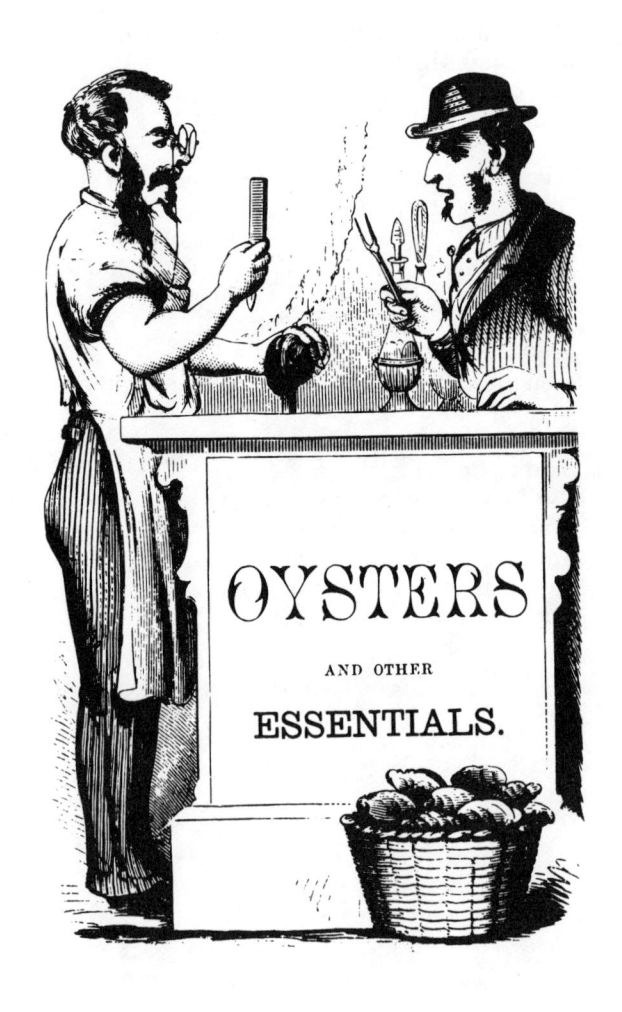

Galivants Ferry
Jimmy Carter Stumped Here
Billed as the "world's largest stump meeting," the Galivants Ferry stump meeting is held the first Monday of May each year at Galivants Ferry on the Pee Dee River and U.S. 501, 18 miles northwest of Conway. This annual get-together began about 100 years ago when political candidates stood on a real stump and laid bare their platforms for being elected to office. Today thousands of people crowd into the parking lot of Pee Dee Farms and General Merchandise Store owned by the Holliday brothers, grandsons of the Holliday who sponsored the first Galivants Ferry Stump. State highway officers direct traffic, and reporters from newspapers and television stations are everywhere. It is considered political suicide for a Democrat to miss the stump meeting in May. As a presidential candidate, Jimmy Carter attended the Galivants Ferry Stump in 1976.

Bailey's Lights
Galivants Ferry was first spelled *Galwants* Ferry, and it is unknown whether the spelling was an error or the way the name was spelled in England. But the story goes that Bailey Galivant was a wealthy man. He slipped away from England to escape a marriage arranged for him to a girl he found unattractive. The first thing he did when he came to this place was to bury gold in a field near the present store. Many tales are told of lights shining over the place where the gold was buried. The mysterious lights that appear deep in the night are called jack-o'-lanterns or Bailey's lights.

The Tobacco Venture
When J. W. Holliday, a man of farsighted conception, came here in 1869, he had an idea that the lowcountry could be fertile in the production of a product that would outshine its former production of indigo, rice and cotton. Some scholars believe that tobacco had been experimented with as early as the seventeenth century in this county, but J. W. Holliday was the first to

cultivate the bright leaf on a large scale. The tobacco venture turned the economy of this county in a new direction. Three generations later, Horry County ranks third in production of flue-cured tobacco of counties worldwide. "The loamy soil produces good tobacco, and we make as good tobacco as is made anywhere in the world," John M. J. Holliday says.

The present generation of Hollidays at Galivants Ferry operate their farms much the way their grandfather did in his day, and what they do not know about tobacco is not worth knowing. They have tenant farmers who come into their stores at Galivants Ferry and Jordanville (JER-don-ville) to requisition, on credit, supplies as they are needed. After the tenant farmers have sold their tobacco, they repay the Hollidays who operate as Pee Dee Farms Corporation. "And we have herds of beef cattle of about 75 or 100 white-faced cattle in a herd," Holliday says. "But we do it more or less because we have the land."

State's Largest Barn

The red barn by U.S. 501 in Galivants Ferry recalls the magnitude of tobacco's earliest years. It is the largest barn in the state. What's more, it has an elevator, although the elevator is used as storage space. In the passageway that runs the length of the barn are traces of the large, tobacco-producing farm owned by the Holliday family. Past the doors on each side of the corridor opening into rooms filled with hay, past a red tractor, past a plow, past the steps leading to the second floor, you come to the back gateway large enough to accommodate motor-driven vehicles which are parked in the hallway when not being used in some stage of tobacco production.

Chicken Bog

Chicken bog was invented in a nearby tobacco barn, and the food cooked by the old-time recipe is sampled by visitors to the May stump meetings.

The story is that a man became hungry as he was keeping watch over a stove in a tobacco barn. The stove was used to keep the barn warm while tobacco leaves were curing. The man obtained chicken from some undisclosed coop and cooked it in a pot on the stove. Just before the chicken was sufficiently cooked, the man added a little rice to the pot. The result was called *chicken bog*.

Galivants Ferry

The Country Store
A saunter through the country store at Galivants Ferry is a treat, and don't fail to notice the *Gone-With-the-Wind*-style mansion near the store.

Bibliography

Allston, Susan Lowndes. *Brookgreen-Waccamaw*. Charleston, S.C.: Southern Printing & Publishing Co., 1956.

Baruch, Bernard M. *Baruch: My Own Story*. New York: Henry Holt and Company, 1957.

Black, J. Gary. *My Friend the Gullah*. Columbia, S.C.: The R.L. Bryan Company, 1974

Bull, Henry DeSaussure. *All Saints' Church, Waccamaw, 1739-1968*. Columbia, S.C.: The R.L. Bryan Company, 1968.

Diaries of George Washington. Boston: Houghton, Mifflin Company, 1925.

Dictionary of American Biography. Biography of Collis P. Huntington. New York: Scribner's, 1932.

Davidson, Chalmers Gaston. *The Last Foray*. Columbia, S.C.: University of South Carolina Press, 1971.

Epps, Florence Theodora. Editor, *The Independent Republic Quarterly*.

Graydon, Nell S. *Eliza of Wappoo*. Columbia, S.C.: The R.L. Bryan Company, 1967.

Lachicotte, Alberta Morel. *Georgetown Rice Plantations*. Columbia, S.C.: The State Printing Company, 1955.

New Century Cyclopedia of Names, vol. 2. New York: Appleton Century Crofts, 1954

Lewis, Oscar. *The Big Four*. New York: Alfred A. Knopf, 1938.

Prevost, Charlotte Kaminski, and Wilder, Effie Leland. *Pawleys Island — A Living Legend*. Columbia, S.C.: The State Printing Company, 1972.

Pringle, Elizabeth Allston. *Chronicles of Chicora Wood*. New York: Scribner's, 1922.

Prooke, Beatrice Gilman. *Archer Milton Huntington*. New York: The Hispanic Society of America, 1963.

Rogers, George C. Jr. *The History of Georgetown County South Carolina*. Columbia, S.C.: University of South Carolina Press, 1970.

Willcox, Clarke R. *Musings of a Hermit*. 3d ed., Charleston, S.C.: Walker, Evans & Cogswell Company, 1968.

Newspapers
Atlanta Constitution
Bridgeport Sunday Post
Charlotte Observer
Georgetown Semi-Weekly Times
Georgetown Times
Horry Herald
Myrtle Beach Sun News
New York Times
San Francisco Examiner

Index

-A-

Africa 85
Aganippe 74
All Saints Church 87
All Saints Church Indulgencies 88
Allen, Tootie 32
Allston, Benjamin 67
    Joseph (1733-1784) 67
    Joseph (1779-1816) 67
    Washington 67
    William 67
Allstons, The 85
Alstons, The 93
America, The Party Ship 24
Arcadia Plantation 91
Arcadian Skyway Golf Course 35
Arcady 42
Army Air Corps 53
Arthur Smith
    King Mackerel Tournament 19
Arundel 64
A. Ruth & Sohn 47
Atalaya 72, 77-79
Atlanta 54
Atlantic Beach 19, 29
Atlantic Beach Civic Center 29
Atlantic Beach Co. 29
Atlantic Coast Line RR 107
Atlantic Coast Lumber Co. 99
Atlantic Ocean 103

-B-

Barrett, A. W. 40
Baruch, Belle 94
Baruch, Bernard 93
Basie, Count 44
Bay Harbor 64
Beach Music 23, 44, 49
Beaty, Mrs. Mary 107
Beese, Welcom 72
Belk, John 49
Belk Stores Services Inc. 49
Bellefield Plantation 94
Bells, The 27
Bermuda 83, 100
Berry, C. B. 27
Bessellieu, George 72
Black Maria 50
Black Panther 54
Black River 95, 101
Blackbeard 61
Bob Collins and the Fabulous Five ... 44
Bonita, The 18
Book Shoppe 48
Boston 18, 100, 114
Boston Red Sox Baseball Club 103, 104
Boundary House 17
Bourbon Street 29
Bristol 100
British, The 95
Brookgreen Gardens 54, 67, 71, 72, 74, 75, 81
Brookgreen Plantation 61, 67, 69, 71, 77
Bryan, George Miller "Buster" 46

Buck, Georgia 112
Buck, Henry 111, 112
Buck, Henry Lee 112
Buck, Jonathan 113
Buck, Lucinda 113
Buck Family Cemetery 113
Bucks Mill 111
Bucksport, Maine 111
Bucksport, S. C. 81, 111, 112
Bucksville 111
Buenos Aires 112
Burr, Aaron 67
    Theodosia 67, 69
Burroughs, Adeline Cooper 40
    D. M. 42
    Edwin 42
    Frank 50
Burroughs & Collins Co. 42

-C-

Cagneys Old Place 48
Campbell, Jim 17
Captain's Bridge 49
Capt. Dick's 64
Caravelle Motor Inn 46
Carolina Shores 17
Carter, Jimmy 115
Cat Island 103
Catalinas, The 44
Chairman of the Board 49
Chandler, Genevieve Willcox 69, 72, 78
Chapin Foundation of Myrtle Beach 42
Chapin Memorial Library 42
Chapin, Simeon B. 33, 40, 42
Charleston 100
Charlotte News 42, 43
Charlotte Observer 43
Cherry Grove Beach 21, 22
Cherry Grove Pier 22
Chicago 42
Chicken Bog 116
Chicora Wood Plantation 64
Churchill, Diana 93
    Sir Winston 93
Civil War 37, 61, 95, 96
Civilian Conservation Corps 51
Clambank Landing 93
Clemson University 71, 94
Coast Guard 43
Coastal Carolina College 91
Coastal Carolina Junior College ... 108, 109
Coastal Education Foundation 108
Connecticut 74
Conway 109
Conway 21, 40, 49, 53, 107-109,
    109, 111, 112, 115
Conway, Robert 107
Conway streets: Fifth Avenue 108
    Gasoline Alley 108
    Lakeside Drive 108
    Main 107
    Racepath Avenue 108

The Grand Strand

Sawdust Road 108
The Gully 108
Third 108
Conwayborough 107
Cooper Store 104
Coquina Club 49
Crescent Beach 25, 27
Cuba 43, 54
Cuban conflict 54
Cypress Swamp 93

— D —

D'Angelo, Jimmy 46
Davidson, Chalmers G. 98
Davidson College 58, 98
Davis' Store 87
Daytona 23
Debordieu Colony Club 91
Department of Defense 53
Detroit Tigers Baseball Club 104
Division of Parks and Recreations 79
Dominican Republic conflict 54
Don Quixote 72
Doolittle, Lt. Col. James 53
Doolittle's Raiders 53
Drunken Jacks 64
Dunbar, Elishua 111
Dunes Golf and Beach Club 37, 38, 46
Dusenbury, Corrie 63

— E —

Emmons, Col. Robert 53
Enterprise 105
Epps, C. J. 40
Ezekiel 27

— F —

Faith Memorial Episcopal Church 72
Floral Beach 57
Flying Fisher 64
Fort Lauderdale 46
Fountain of the Muses 74
Freeman, W.A. 40
Friendfield House 93
Friendfield Village 93
Frye, Toby 18

— G —

Gabreski, Col. Francis 54
Galivant, Bailey 115
Galivants Ferry 57, 115-117
Galivants Ferry Stump Meeting 115
Galwants Ferry 115
Garden City Beach 59, 79
Gause family 31
Gause Swash 31
Gause, William 31
Gause's Place 31
Gay Dolphin Gift Shop 48
George II 95
Georgetown 63, 67, 74, 77, 91, 93, 95,
96-101

Georgetown Chamber of Commerce . . . 101
Georgetown County 35, 59
Georgetown Semi-Weekly Times 39
Georgetown Steel Corporation 100
Georgetown streets: Broad 95, 97, 101
Cannon 96, 97
Front 97, 98, 101
High Market 95, 97, 101
King 97
Orange 97
Prince 96
Queen 97
St. James 97
Screven 97
South Island Road . 104
Georgetown Times 99
Georgetown Tour Train 101
Germany 47
Golf Boom 46
Golf Hill 32
Golf Holiday 46
Gore's Motel 29
Goss Swash 31
Goudett, Peter 100
Grand Strand . . 31, 43, 46, 53, 54, 59, 67, 83
Great Depression 29, 43, 72, 77, 99
Great Dismal Swamp 35, 42
Greece 42
Greenville 42
Grove Hill Plantation 81
Gullah 81
Gullyfield 48

— H —

Hagley Plantation 89, 95
Hammock Shop 89
Hasell Hill Plantation 81
Hasty Point 64
Haul Seining 29
Hawaiian Village 48
Hebron Methodist Church 111, 112
Henrietta, The 111, 112
Henry, Patrick 35
Heriot, Edward 63
Heriots, The 93
Herman, Woody 44
Hidden Village 48
Hobcaw Barony 93, 94
Hobcaw House 93
Hojo Lounge 48
Holliday family 115
Holliday, George 57
John M. J. 115, 116
J. W. 115
Holly Hill Plantation 81
Hood, Raymond, M. 42
Horry, Ben 59
Horry County 35, 59, 105-107, 111, 116
Horry County
Higher Education Commission 108
Horry County Museum 109
Horry-Georgetown Technical College . 108
Horry-Marion-Georgetown
Technical Education Center 108
Horry Herald 38, 43
Howard Johnson's Resort Inn 48
Hugers, The 93

Index

Huguenot Church, Charleston 97
Huntington, Anna Hyatt 54, 67,
                    69, 72, 74, 77, 78
    Archer Milton 67, 69, 72, 74, 77
    Collis P. 67, 74
Huntington Beach State Park 77-79
Huntington Beach
    State Park Campground 79
Huntingtons, The 69, 71
Hurl Rock Beach 49
Hurricane, The 18
Hurricane Hazel 21, 31, 44

—I—

India 33
Ink Spots 44
International Paper Corp. 99
Intracoastal Waterway .. 17, 35, 49, 81, 105
Island Shops 88
Island Queen II 64

—J—

Jackson, Major 31
Jennewein, C. Paul 72
Jonah 49
Jordan, Daniel W. 21
        I. C. 27
Jordanville 116
Joyner, Robert L. 103, 104

—K—

Kaminski, Julia 98
        Harold 98
Kaminski House 98
Kaminskis, The 98
King Mackerel Tournament 19
Kingston Presbyterian Church 108
Kits Pier 31
Knox, Dorothy 42
Kobe, Yokahama 112

—L—

Labruces, The 85
Lachicotte, A. H. 88
        A. H. "Doc," Jr. 88
Lake Arrowhead Road 37
Landmark 49
Last Foray, The 98
Laurel Hill 67, 69
Lebanon conflict 54
Lewises, The 27
Lexington, Battle of 17
Litchfield Beach 83, 84
Litchfield Plantation 83, 84
Little, E. H. Library, Davidson College ... 98
Little River 17, 18, 19, 31
Lombardo, Guy 44
London 69, 100
Long Bay 25
Lords Proprietors 93
Louisville 19
Low Country Stores 66
Lower Mill 111
Lynch, Thomas, Sr. 96

—M—

Magic Mushroom 32
Magic Shop 32
Maine 111
Manhattan Guest House 29
Marine Laboratory 93
Marion, Francis 17, 67, 107
        Gabriel 67
        Isaac 17
Marsh Harbour Golf Club 17
Marthas Vineyard 47
Maxwell, Walter 22
Meher Baba 33
Meher Spiritual Center 33, 34
Melbourne, Australia 112
Metropolitan Museum of Art 75
Miami Beach 59
Middle Mill 111
Milles, Carl 74
Mills Brothers 44
Mills, Robert 107
Minor, James 21
Minor's Island 21
Mole Hole 89
Montgomery, Bob 40
Morrall, John 61
Mosier 69, 77, 78
Mount Arena Plantation 81
Mt. Olympus 24
Murrells Inlet 59, 61, 64, 66, 67, 69, 82
Myrtle Beach 33, 37, 39-51, 53, 54,
                    85, 95, 106, 107-109
Myrtle Beach Air Force Base .. 32, 51, 54, 58
Myrtle Beach Army Air Field 53
Myrtle Beach Convention Center 47
Myrtle Beach Farms Co. 42, 47
Myrtle Beach Hilton 48
Myrtle Beach Pavilion 47
Myrtle Beach State Park 51, 53
Myrtle Beach Mall 48

—N—

Nags Head 69
National Register
    of Historic Places 75, 85, 95, 108, 112
Nautilus Shop 32
New England 59, 111, 112
New Inlet Princess 64
New Orleans 19, 29
New Rascal 18
New Town 40
New York 54, 67, 93, 111
New York City 78
Nichols, Captain Jonathan 111
Nixon family 21
Nixon, Nicholas F. 21
North Carolina 35
North Jetty 59, 79
North Island 103
North Myrtle Beach 19, 21, 29, 35

—O—

"O.D." 23
Oak Hampton Plantation 81
Oak Lawn Plantation 81
Oaks, The 67

121

The Grand Strand

Ocean Drive Beach 23, 24
Ocean Dunes, The 48
Ocean Forest Hotel 42, 43, 44, 47
Ocean Forest Villas 47
Ocean Pier Condominiums 31
Old Slave Market 95
Old Town 40
Oliver's Lodge 64, 66
Oregon Plantation 105, 106
Outlet Park 49
O Zion 85

— P —

Pad, The 23
Pate, Mrs. Wallace 91
Patriot, The 67, 69
Patterson, Elizabeth 33
Pawley, Anthony 85
        George 85, 87
        Percival I 85
Pawleys Island 72, 85-89, 91
Pawleys Island Inn 88
Pawleys Pier Village 86
Pearl Beach 29
Pee Dee Farms Corp. 115, 116
Pee Dee River 31, 85, 95, 101, 115
Pelican Inn 89
Pequin Boutique 66
Perrin, J. W. 27
Piedmont Airlines 54
Pilot House 66
Pine Island Cut 105
Pine Lakes International Country Club . . 42
Pipe Down Plantation 81
Plantation Square 112
Planters Back Porch 66
Plyler, Justin 48
Ponderosa 32
Poole 100
Pope's Place 23
Portland, Oregon 111
Prince George Winyah Church 95, 101
Prince of Wales 95
Pyatts, The 98

— R —

Rainbow Harbor 48
Randall, Thomas 19
Randall-Vereen House 18, 19
Restaurant Row 48
Revolutionary War 23, 95
Rhode Island 42
Rice Museum 95
Road's End 112
Rochester, Massachusetts 19
Rocinante 72
Roll, Jordan, Roll 85
Ron Tom Marina 19
Roosevelt, Franklin D. 51, 93, 94
Ross, Captain Andrew M. 111
Ruinville Plantation 81
Russell, Richard 39

— S —

St. John's Inn 49
St. Mary's Chapel 95
Sampit River 95, 98, 100, 101, 104
Sancho Panza 72
Sand Dollar Squares 29
Sand Dunes, The 48
Sandy Island 64, 81, 82
Sandy Knowe Plantation 81
Santee River 101
Savannah 18
Scotland 78
Sculptured Oak Nature Trail 51
Sea Captain's House 66
Seaside Inn 40
Shag 44
Sheraton 49
Sherwood Forest 32
Shore Road 37
Simons, John 83
        Peter 83
Singapore 112
Singletons Swash 37, 38
Skene, Alexander 107
Slug's Rib 48
Smith, Arthur 19
Smith, Benjamin 17
Smith, Jeremiah 105
Socastee 82, 105, 106
Socastee Academy 106
Socastee General Merchandise Store . . . 106
S. C. Council 22
S. C. Hall of Fame 47
S. C. Wildlife and
   Marine Resources Dept. 103
S. C. Wildlife Sanctuary 34
South Jetty 79
South Island 103
South's Old Guard 42
Southern Assn. of Colleges and Schools 109
Southern Pacific Railway 67
Spain 54
Spillane, Mickey 64
Springfield Plantation 67
Springs, Col. Holmes B. 42
Stevens, Mayor Cleveland 29
Straw Cove 48
Sunnyside Plantation 61
Surfside Beach 57, 58
Swamp Fox Roller Coaster 49
Swash Boats 32

— T —

Tarbox, Frank G. Jr. 71
Teach, Edward (Blackbeard) 61
Temple of Dionysus 87
Tennis 46
Thompson, James C. 71
Thunderbolt II 53
Tilghman's Point 19
Tito and Rogers 77
Toby's Old World 18
Tokyo 53
Tourist Welcome Center 17
Town Hall and Clock, Keswick, England . 95
Train Depot,
   Village of the Barefoot Traders 32
Tribune Tower Building 42
Trinity Episcopal Church, Columbia 97

Index

Tucker, Daniel 83
Tuckers, The 85
Turtle Lounge 49
Tyson, George 29

—U—

University of S. C. 94, 108
University of S. C. Press 98
Upper Mill 111

—V—

Vanderbilt, George 91
Vereen Family Cemetary 18
Vereen, Jeremiah 37
Vereen Memorial Historical Gardens 18
Vereen's Marina 24
Village of the Barefoot Traders 32
Virginia 35

—W—

Wacca Wache Marina 64, 82
Waccamaw Pottery 49
Waccamaw River 19, 31, 50, 61, 77
      81, 83, 95, 101, 105, 111, 112
Waccamaw River Tours 64, 82
Wachesaw Plantation 61, 63, 106
Wall, E. Craig, Sr. 43
War of 1812 19
Ward, Joshua John 69, 71, 88
Ward, R. V. 29
Wards, The 27, 85, 87
Washington, George 17, 18, 31, 35, 37
Washington Monument 108
Waterway Hills 35
Waties Island 19
Wayne, John 64
West Indies 67, 96
Weston, Plowden C. J. 87, 89, 95
Westons, The 85
White, Edward Brickell 97
White Point Swash 31
Williams, Maurice 49
Wilmington, Chadbourn & Conway Line 107
Windy Hill Beach 31-33, 48
Windy Hill Pier 31
Winyah Academy 96
Winyah Bay 93, 95, 103
Winyah Indigo Society Hall . . 69, 96, 97, 101
Wisconsin 42
Woodland 61, 63
Woodside, John T. 42
Woodsides, The 42
World Exposition (1900) 47
World War II 53, 83
Wright, Chief Justice 107
Wurlitzer 165 Band Organ 47

—Y—

Yachtsman complex 49
Yawkey, Tom 103, 104
Yawkey Wildlife Center 103, 104

Other travelers from The East Woods Press

Carolina Seashells, Nancy Rhyne, $4.95 paper. "For the summer beachcomber, Nancy Rhyne's practical, instructive *Carolina Seashells* just might be the perfect book to carry along to the coast." *The Columbia State*

Tar Heel Sights, Guide to North Carolina's Heritage, Marguerite Schumann, $8.95 paper. "Includes more than 1,000 historical and cultural sites statewide." *Southern Living*

Blue Ridge Mountain Pleasures: An A-Z Guide to North Georgia, Western North Carolina and the Upcountry of South Carolina, Donald C. Wenberg, $8.95 paper. This one-of-its-kind guide lists more than 1,500 exciting events and activities, most of which are low-cost or free.

Southern Guest House Book, Corinne Madden Ross, $7.95 paper. Charming and diverse establishments, mostly bed and breakfast, in the historic South.

Carolina Curiosities: Jerry Bledsoe's Outlandish Guide to the Dadblamedest Things to See and Do in North Carolina, Jerry Bledsoe, $7.95 paper. "You will learn things about Tarheelia you've never known before . . ." *Southern Pines Pilot*

Just Folks: Visitin' with Carolina People, Jerry Bledsoe, $9.95 hardcover. "Jerry Bledsoe is Carolina's Listener Laureate. Nobody beats him at listening to the human voice and to the human heart, and nothing beats holding his book in your hands and listening with him." Charles Kuralt, *CBS News*

Copies of these and other East Woods Press books are available from your bookseller or directly from The East Woods Press, 429 East Boulevard, Charlotte, NC 28203. (704) 334-0897. For orders **only,** call toll free (800) 438-1242, in NC (800) 532-0476. Visa, MasterCard and checks accepted. Ask for our FREE catalog.